A Pillow ON THE Highway

A Pillow ON THE Highway

FINDING REST

BILLIE CASH

AMBASSADOR INTERNATIONAL

GREENVILLE, SOUTH CAROLINA & BELFAST, NORTHERN IRELAND

A PILLOW ON THE HIGHWAY
FINDING REST

All scriptures used are quoted from the NIV unless noted in Pillow Notes.

Cover design & page layout by A&E Media — David Siglin

ISBN 978 1 932307 80 1

Published by the Ambassador Group

Ambassador Emerald International
427 Wade Hampton Blvd.
Greenville, SC 29609 USA
www. emeraldhouse.com

and

Ambassador Publications Ltd.
Providence House
Ardenlee Street
Belfast BT6 8QJ
Northern Ireland
www. ambassador-productions.com

The colophon is a trademark of Ambassador

DEDICATION

To:

Audrey McClung, Evie Buehring, Annette Hunt, Sandy Presnell, Ella Poplin,
Nancy Stone, Barbara Buckelew, Judy Tressel, Jan Kellett, Nita Keim,
Peggy Davis, Kate Roll, Peggy McGaha,
Beth Kelly, Hope Roberts, Stephanie Carbaugh

You have journeyed the highway of faith with me and
pillowed my life in prayer.

**And the song from beginning to end
I found again in the heart of a friend.**

Henry Wadsworth Longfellow

A FRIEND LOVES AT ALL TIMES

Proverbs 17:17

They were strangers in the world but near and familiar to God.

Thomas A. Kempis

ENDORSEMENTS

Christ's middle cry of victory on the cross was, in the Gospel text, a single word, telestai. It means 'it has been and will forever remain finished.' In this unique book Billie Cash shows us that Christ's mighty finished work opens to us a rest that our frantic modern world will never deliver. In a deeply creative and most refreshing way Billie draws her reader out after this awesomely available rest. Here is comfort for the suffering, wisdom for the busy, insight for the thoughtful and inspiration on every page.

Derek Bingham
Adjunct professor of English Literature, John Brown University, AR
Lecturer, prolific author
Belfast, Ireland

Billie powerfully writes once again drawing her readers to seek and experience spiritual truth. This time it is God's rest. An effective communicator and dear friend she personally unfolds a life of balance that voices love, strength and joy.

Dale Buehring
President
Crown Ministries, International
Apache Junction, Arizona

I enjoyed reading and recapturing in your thoughts once again my love and passion for JESUS. I pray that all who read it will also experience the love of Christ...immediately and powerfully.

Wendy Muendler
Daughter in Christ, mother of Maya and Lucy
Oberreichenbach, Germany

Your book is inspiring and your style of writing unique and poetic. By using simple things and situations all around us to describe God's abundant and gracious providence, we discover we can truly rest in and trust in our God, who is our pillow.

Mark Gollop
Dorset, England

In A Pillow on the Highway, Billie reminds us that when we relinquish control in our lives we find God revealing the rest HE has promised. Billie thrills us with His Sovereignty while encouraging us with His comfort.

Peggy McGaha
Women's ministry
Papillion, Nebraska

Your book has a simple message but a BIG truth. Find rest in God. In chapter Three you said, "We build altars for ourselves to catch up, sleep-in, play up, vegetate or let down. We are exhausted and spent because we have forgotten HIM...the altar of me is exhausting." How true. The chapters are honest vignettes which pull out truth from God's Word. Your book is a refreshing view of life lived out, lived in, and resting in Jesus Christ. A *Pillow on the Highway* caused me to ask where the good way is and then purpose to walk in it.

Shea Portman
Mom to Sami and Caylin,
Hillsborough, North Carolina

Billie writes in a way in which all women can identify. This book is both inspiring and comforting. God's Word leaps from its pages. I loved it.

Tomi Beckemeyer
Medical Aesthetician
Memphis, Tennessee

I will never look at REST the same way again. Jeremiah 6:16 will always remind me of your life and love of Jesus but most of all I will be cognizant of this truth; true rest will be mine as long as I walk with HIM.

Patricia Sellers
Avid reader, walker, sister in faith
Bahama, North Carolina

Your chapters are eloquent, insightful and full of grace-led words of encouragement. The stories you share are endearing and will touch the heart of every woman who reads them. Thank you, Billie. This book "watered my soul."

Cora R. Blinsmon
Writer, traveler, mom
Durham, North Carolina

This book will minister to others whatever their need or circumstance. It has caused me to look to Jesus reminding me of His faithfulness. I pray your readers will hear God speak to them through your openness and transparency. It has been a joy to read.

Pat Maxwell
Grandmother of six, great grandmother of three, prayer partner.
Germantown, Tennessee

A *Pillow on the Highway* is calming, restful....devotional.

Pam Speien
Minnetoka, Minnesota

A Pillow on the Highway is a strong message about how we have lost our way. The picture is the story of our lives. Each chapter brings us back to the only true rest, surrender, daily surrender to the sovereignty of God!

Peggy Davis
Author, teacher, prayer mentor, beloved friend
Virginia Beach, Virginia

The message of this book will encompass all readers. In one of Billie's stories she writes about robins building a nest and birthing their young. The wonder of life in them was translated into the gift of life in me. Provision is rest and it has been written by one of God's beautiful servants, Billie Cash, Thank you. I pray we will all find our "Pillow on the Highway."

Teressa Gamble
Wife to John, mother to Alise and John Ridgell, runner
Charleston, South Carolina

A Pillow on the Highway richly draws us into God's presence. Billie captures the true experience of surrender and acknowledges the splendor of God's glory. Thank you Billie, for keeping us on course and driving us ahead in our journey of living in the Word of God. The only real solace found amongst the busyness and the brokenness of this world is God's Word for it is the answer to our every need, our resting place.

Jan Fugler
Director of Women's Ministries at West Bowles Community Church
Littleton, Colorado

Billie lives what she writes. In *A Pillow on the Highway*, she is walking through the crushing experience of her mother's descent into physical frailty and dementia. This book is a syllabus on surviving and overcoming circumstances that can overwhelm and destroy us. Read it and weep, read it and conquer, read it and prevail in the face of your darkness as you learn to rest in Christ alone.

Jim Meyer; D.D.S
Memphis, Tennessee

In *A Pillow on the Highway*, I cried and laughed as I pictured your walk in the rain with the Lord for I was reminded that God's rain "washes away the toxins of fear and fatigue" in my life. The picture of the earthworms coming up for air when it rains because moisture is the vehicle that helps them cross over the hard concrete to the other side is just what I needed. God allows the rain to get me to the other side. As Billie communicated, His path requires radical devotion, surrender and then rest comes.

Denise Turner
Mom to three sons, Bible teacher, faithful praying friend.
Germantown, Tennessee

God comforts us in our trials so we may comfort others and that is what Billie does with her Holy Spirit-anointed words. Sometimes it seems we have a stone for a pillow but "recognizing God's presence," she "pours oil" on the hard place making it a memorial to God's faithfulness. Her words have served to make my own "stone pillow" a sweeter place.

A.R. Bruno
Senor Editor, Christian Audio
San Diego, California

Children are at peace when those who care for them have learned to rest in God's loving presence. I know this because long before my mother wrote this book I saw her live its truth. How many times as a little boy did I awaken to find her on her knees before God? How many times did she return from a solitary walk beaming even in the midst of turmoil and crossroads. With my father deployed in the Navy and often in harm's way ours was a life of constant change and crossroads. A *Pillow on the Highway* is a living breathing exposition of Jeremiah 6:16 which brings into the brightest focus what the author has lived for decades and what God Almighty intends each of us to experience every day...a treasure of truth and testimony that will transform your life.

LCDR Carey Cash, US Navy Chaplain
Author of best seller, A *Table in the Presence*
Naples, Italy

SCRIPTURE PAGE

"STAND AT THE CROSSROADS AND LOOK. ASK FOR THE
ANCIENT PATHS. ASK WHERE THE GOOD WAY IS AND WALK
IN IT AND YOU WILL FIND REST FOR YOUR SOULS."
Jeremiah 6:16

ACKNOWLEDGEMENTS

Praying Friends, your prayer covering has been a pillow on the highway for me. You have carried me through an intense period of change and resolve in my life.

Thank you Ann, Denise, Pat and Joyce for understanding the call I have in ministry and continuing to respond ever so faithfully.

A special thanks to my inner circle – Peggy, Audrey, Beth, Peggy "in the cornfields", Hope and Stephanie – who pray me through every thing I do. You are in my heart forever.

I also want to thank all those read the manuscript and made suggestions and comments; in particular Pat Thomas, Pat Russell, Dr. Roz Payne, Antonino Bruno and Wendy Stutzel.

Bless you, wonderful internet base, which is scattered all over the world. When prayer alerts go out, you pray and God answers.

I am thankful for a new church home, the Galilean Class, and the beginning of some precious new praying friendships. How faithful is God.

A blessed thanks to my husband for his mastery in editing, and to my publishers Sam and Tim Lowry.

I have spent time in the trenches of fatigue.
I have climbed out of the pit to stand on God's Word.
I have gleaned great solace from rediscovery.
I have learned to rest in the midst of misery and marvel.
I am reclaimed once again.

Thank you, Lord for equipping me to write and experience the Rest of God.
Bless my praying friends as they learn the lessons of leaning and weaning.
May they find YOUR rest on the highway.

Billie Cash

TABLE OF CONTENTS

FOREWORD

"Rest is not a hallowed feeling that comes over us in church; it is the response of a heart set deep in God," writes Henry Drummond (as quoted in Streams in the Desert, 1959)

How does one gain a heart set deep in God? In *A Pillow on the Highway*, Billie Cash answers this question by pointing to Jeremiah 6:16.

1. Stand at the crossroads.
2. Walk in the way God directs.
3. Ask for the ancient compass.

As she develops these three steps, she weaves into her writing the principles of God-given rest.

Rest will almost always involve the laying down of one's attempt to control, to make things happen. To the heart whose sin is washed away, rest will come. Rest will come from taking up new and creative endeavors for God, whereas those things that fatigue and stress stifle one's attempt to rest. Furthermore, rest will be initiated with the heart's cry to God for help. Rest will point to a faith-filled trust. We conclude that, all in all, the obedient heart is the rested heart.

In a culture where a frantic search for relief from concern and grasping desire dominates the days, *A Pillow on the Highway* points to rest that is complete.

Thank you, Billie Cash, for writing this book.

Judy Chatham
Greenwood, Indiana
July 8, 2007

PREFACE

As I lifted the forgotten music box from its resting place atop my china cabinet to begin the process of packing for a move, a deluge of memory met me as the enchanting music of *Memories*, from the musical, *Cats*, cast its spell.
A keen poignancy swept through my senses, evoking restlessness.
A flow from the past rushed in as a flood of the future loomed.
My eyes fell upon the artistic, porcelain, sculptured rendering of a mother bird positioned to feed her two babies who were eagerly anticipating their next meal. The musical refrain soon ended but the still life before me became alive with real life truth.
Here's what I saw:
The little family was surrounded in beauty, as palest blue morning glories draped themselves along the side of each bird, framing each picturesquely.
The mother bird was resting on a perch, perfectly poised to feed them.
The babies were pillowed in a nest with their beaks lifted up, ready.
This Norman Rockwell scene was an impression of child-like trust and confidence.
The more I looked, the more I saw.
It was an epiphany, a God-awareness awakening within me a longing for HIM.
Being wooed by my heavenly Father, I had been compelled to stop what I was doing, pause, look and remember.
Before me was a visual reminder of abundant provision, so I stopped my cleaning and packing and laid down my work.
Mesmerized, as though a pied piper had sung to me, I picked up the music box and walked upstairs to the computer.
I was stirred to sit down and write out what I had internalized.
God wants to mirror life for us, His life in little serendipities.
Today I saw where I needed to go.
Whatever task lies in my hands must be entrusted daily unto HIM because this is the ancient way, the good way.

"Stand in the crossroads, and look; ask for the ancient paths. Ask where the good way is, and walk in it, and you will find rest for your souls." Jeremiah 6:16

I am to stand, look, ask and walk in this way.
I am to believe there will be ample supply.
I am to look expectantly.
I am to know HE will come.
Overwhelmed at the imminent undertaking before me of moving once again, I saw HE was ahead of me orchestrating the next step.
HE is ahead of you too, ahead of every anxiety, loss, set back, disappointment, weakness and fatigue.
HE will surprise you if you will look for Him.
I returned my music box to the dining room where I had to resume the packing, but my weariness had evaporated.
I had found rest in HIM.
You see, this is an ancient path that HE has been pointing to since the beginning of time.
It is there, available if we are.

Lord, I need rest for my soul today.
I am available.
YOU come.
With increased awareness I will seek the good way found in Your Word.
I surrender the unknowns for the KNOWN – YOU.
Because of Jesus I accept the confident provision that is mine in the midst of the uncertain and chaotic.
In His Beloved Surety, I rest.

Billie Cash WINTER 2006-2007

Chapter One

CROSSROADS FAITH

Crossroads come.

Faith watches.

It was a humid, suffocating, bone-dry July and I found myself staring emotionally at a self-imposed fork in the road.

I felt a stifling urgency.

My choice was to retreat or advance.

An intense pressure was building within and an unbearable Memphis summertime heat choked me.

Physical weakness stalked me and time was evaporating like my resolve.

A deadline was hanging.

Yes, I was at a crossroad.

I needed a viable solution.

How could I get this writing project completed by the end of August?

I uttered a cry, "Lord, YOU know the way. Show me YOUR way," I prayed.

HE did.

Since I was already walking in the mornings for about thirty minutes to build my stamina, I had the distinct impression that I was to stretch my walking time to an hour.

That's a long walk for our summers.

Wondering if I could, I began by walking 45 minutes and then working up to an hour.

In order to endure the humidity, it had to be predawn walking.

Cooler, quieter, less distractions.

Waking up and walking early while it was still dark was the way, the plan.

I trekked out my door, armed with an ID card (in case something happened to me), keys to my house, and a seeker's faith.

The path for my walking was interesting because it led me through a huge complex of apartments with single dwellings surrounding it, designed with hills and valleys, sharp turns and bordering intersections. In fact, I had to cross over a busy artery every day, normally traveled by commuters, but disarmingly silent and void of traffic now. There was lush green landscaping to observe, which was constantly being refurbished every day by workers busily preparing their day's gardening chores in order to keep the planted beds healthy and thriving. Full, dense oak trees with garden spots strategically scattered throughout were welcomed oases – day lilies in shades of spicy tangerine and creamed yellow softened the corners of the buildings. A man-made pond carefully sculpted in the center of this maze of buildings and edged by fieldstones in shades of brick tan, mossy covered beige and weathered caramel skirted a noisy waterfall cascading over a high knoll.

Those who lived around the pond woke up to this refreshing sound.

This picturesque place was music to me, a reward for climbing the hill.

How I wanted to stay there and just listen to the rushing water.

It gave my soul a shower as God began to water my parched faith.

I then left the pond scene and began to walk up the other side of the hill. The first rays of luminous morning light streaked across the heavens, spreading before me the sun's gloriously opening smile upon the day. Glints of luminous aqua and fiery hues of apricot ran together, framed by a few wisps of ivory cloud cover hanging like cotton candy, fragile and easily dissipated. It is a subtle but profound experience to be walking in the dark and then to experience the lifting of night and the awakening of day, ever so gently almost stealing into the human psyche by degrees, bringing focus. It is as though a veil has parted without knowing when or how it did.

Night and day are separate but they flow from each other.

They meet.

In this daily ritual of a walking stillness, my bodily strength was renewed, creativity surged, beauty was observed and refreshment was received.

A sharp awareness came one morning as I began to observe what people had thrown away, discarded or unknowingly lost during the previous day or night.

Trash, if you will.

I noticed the trash.

Why?

Because it had been scattered along my path, my route, and sometimes in my way. I would almost trip over some of it or my eye would take notice because, as light emerged, I could finally see more clearly.

And I saw more than trash.

The objects which were revealed by early morning light were a reflection of the focus of our lives today, our frantic attempts to find relief, consuming and throwing away, and then starting over, valuing nothing.

Over the course of these morning jaunts, this is what I observed:

There were coins, a driver's license, food wrappers, empty bottles, a nail, a furniture tag, a child's blue shirt, keys, a banana peel, a ball, and underwear – even a # 13 billiard ball.

My heart was curiously troubled at the possible significance of this refuse.

This was a Pandora's Box.

I began to ponder on what they might represent to our worn out minds.

For within us all, there seems to be a search for something we don't have, a yearning to feel whole, a desire to value something, to be filled up with enough.

What compels us to trash life?

Is it something we had once and lost along the way or something we never found?

I mulled over these findings every morning, imagining the people who had pitched them out a car window or thrown them on the street.

As I returned home something stirred my own conscience.

I questioned what I was aimlessly throwing away, using up, consuming.

What was my trash?

The pressure of the impending deadline had become my tyranny of the urgent.

I craved increased stamina for the demanding assignment ahead but I was also longing for rest.

The way to rest is not a reward from more self-effort.

The way to rest is God ordained, initiated from the heart's cry for help.

The way to rest is a life style of giving and receiving from HIM.

Who?

Our God.

So I would arrive home from my walk, wondrously able, empowered, spiritually flowing with words that my Heavenly Father had placed in me, filled with more love for HIM than ever before, energized to write, charged with fresh thoughts about many things not considered before.

And there was rest.

Why?

Because I had been with HIM.

HE was my exclusive companion on these morning sojourns.

Returning home, hungrily I scoffed down my breakfast and bounded upstairs to the computer to write down and preserve what I had received that day.

These thoughts, images, scriptures would become the foundation for this book.

You mean that my overwhelmed, anxious heart that was frenzied to find a way to "finish the present project on time" discovered more time, more creativity, more joy, more reverence for life, more rest?

Yes.

Did I have the same number of hours I had the day before?

Yes.
Could I expect to have enough of what I needed to complete what I had started?
Yes.
Why?
Because the God of the Universe is calling us to rest in HIM,
And guess what?
HE called me.

...all of the promises of God in Him are Yes and in Him Amen, to the glory of God through us. (1)

God has some "yeses" for us.

Eye has not seen, nor ear heard, nor entered into the heart of man the things which God has prepared for those who love Him. (2)

And there is an Amen.

It is the heart that yearns for rest that finds it in Him alone.

Rest for our work, a settled sense of direction, a faith fervor found in Him.

...I will guide you with my Eye. (3)

He is watching us.

Rest for sleep, for bodies spent in seeking.

He giveth his beloved sleep. (4)

Our fatigue is fueled through an intense desire to control.
Our faith is weakened by marathon managing.
Our future is secured by the sure Hand of a Loving God who KNOWS the WAY, "the good way" and waits for us to choose it.
Finding the path to rest is a quest but it is not foreign to saints of previous generations, to the men and women in the Bible,
And it is available to you and me.
Hallelujah!

As the sun finally soared into the heavens one tepid morning on my walk, my eyes spied a crumpled looking heap in the shadows.

It was a pillow.

Someone had lost their pillow.

Pillows soften life, support our head and neck, bring comfort and, yes, they are a symbol of rest.

It was then I knew the title of this book, A *Pillow on the Highway*.

How we long to stop the clock, to breathe in invigorating possibility, to absorb nature's gift of creation without interruption.

We have created treadmill faith.

God wants us to have a resting faith.

Today HE is present.

Are we?

And He is calling us to rest.

We need a pillow on the highway and He will bring it to us so we can take the next step.

The scripture says that there is glory from God to be declared through us.

Declare his glory among the nations.... (5)

Can you imagine that?

Aren't you weary just trying to live?

How can we embrace this truth?

Sometimes don't you want to just lie down and not get up?

Have you lost your pillow?

Or have you found the resting place of belonging to the Living God so that HE can direct you along the way, HIS Way?

There is a hopelessness that stalks us and frustrates our way until we eliminate the excess.

There is a daily whisper to pursue HIM – to find His rest.

Do you know that you know HE is there?

If you don't know that you know, you probably don't know.

How can you know?

The Crossroads of faith comes through the Cross to us.

Every day.

Why?

Because The Cross cancels the depravity in our lives if we believe and receive Jesus.

To do so we must cease trashing our own way.

We must stop at the crossroads.

Jesus came to make a Way.

HIS Way works.
HIS Blood was the sacrifice opening our lives to the rest we have dreamed of
and desired.

"Have you ever learned the beautiful art of letting God take care of you?
It will relieve you of a thousand cares."
A.B. Simpson

We begin with faith.
A refrain from an old hymn says it best;

My faith has found a resting place not in device or creed.
It is enough that Jesus died and that He died for me.
I need no other argument.
I need no other plea.
It is enough that Jesus died and that HE died for me.

Faith is born in the heart and then it must find a resting place
Every day.

I needed rest to continue to believe that God was ahead of me in this project.
You may need faith to believe HE loves you.
When we surrender our agenda HE comes.

"When we run a race…it is easy to become short of breath. Rest is to our inner
life what air is to our lungs. The life of God is the air we breathe to revive us.
When we receive God's rest…quietness comes…calm…stillness." (6)

We find our pillow in Jesus' loving arms.
Every day.

ARRESTING THOUGHTS:

1.   Why do I run from the concept of God's rest?

2.   Can I know that I am accepted by Him just as I am?

3.   Is it possible to lay down my past before Him and rest in His plans?

REST ASSURED

So shall the world be created each morning anew, forgiven – in Thee, by Thee.
– Dag Hammarskjold

A PILLOW PRAYER

Father of Love;
I need a father, a friend, a comfort, a refuge.
Is it possible that YOU have known all along what I was racing to find was waiting for me?
I have tried to conjure up my own rest and have come up empty.
I have not known that faith was the crossroads of my beginning.
The Cross of Jesus was the marker.
HE came for me.
His blood was shed for my vain attempts to fill up my own life.
My sin has obliterated rest.
Now I come into faith and ask for the Love of Jesus to become real to me,
To become my resting place, to live in me.
I ask for forgiveness.
Cleanse me now from the self-effort which has separated me from YOU.
I do believe.
I now receive.
I promise to cleave to YOU.
I will rest in God alone.
Remind me when I step away from the Way.
Bring me back every time to my resting place in Jesus.
I now KNOW that I KNOW I am His forever, His child.

Chapter Two
STANDING TO LOOK

To look is to investigate.
Faith ponders.

Are you tired of always trying to get somewhere but never arriving?
What does *rest* look like to the world?
Is it an attempt to add or subtract something from what is?
An overstressed woman is a danger.
Fatigue is a reality.
Trampoline living isn't working.
"Stress is linked to physical and mental health, as well as decreased willingness to take on new and creative endeavors.... A recent Roper Starch Worldwide Survey of 30,000 people between the ages of 13 and 65 in 30 countries concluded that women who work fulltime and have children under the age of 13 report the greatest stress worldwide.... Depression, only one type of stress reduction, is predicted to be the leading occupational disease of the 21st century." (1)
So we must stand up and look at the facts.
Women and men are experiencing burn out.
Stress management is a 21st century discipline, but experts argue that this phenomenon is predominately limited to North America.
"Burnout is the dislocation between what people are and what they have to do.... It represents an erosion of values, dignity, spirit and will – an erosion of the human soul...." (2)
So we must take an honest look within.
Our mental and physical lives are being compromised.
Our emotional well being is not well.
Our spiritual focus is out of focus.
Women are worn out.
God is not.
Is HE pleading with us to STOP?
In God's Word we are admonished to stop.
Are you tired? Worn out? Burned out on religion? Come to me...get away with me

and you'll recover your life. I'll show you how to take a real rest...watch how I do it. Learn the unforced rhythms of grace...keep company with me and you'll learn to live freely and lightly. (3)

We are crying out for balance, space, time – rest.
Our faith is fainting.

Come unto me all you who are weary and carry burdens, and I will give you rest. Let me teach you... (4)
Perfunctory, duty bound lip service faith won't do.
We have to stand up and seek the Master.
Our souls need rest.
Is this search a new thing?
In Arthur Miller's screen play, *The Misfits*, we look at some characters that mirror this ongoing dilemma.
Disappointment, diversion and deluded dreams are the stuff that makes movies memorable.
Why?
Because in them we see ourselves.
This story unravels the death of an era, the old west, and is a penetrating look at the cowboy lifestyle.
What was their daily expectation?
Expedient lives used up on the road, free from commitments, working rodeos – just enough food, clothing, shelter and drink to get by.
A few bucks will do for today.
The story goes like this: three men and two women are thrown together in this slice of life.
Clark Gable plays the character, Gay, an aging, robust and rugged cowboy with a disarming smile who is always on the hunt for adventure.
He has two broken, scrappy cohorts, Guido and Perce. Guido, played by Eli Wallach, is a widower who loves to fly airplanes. He provides the unfinished, half built house in the desert of Nevada which is the backdrop of the movie.
This is where they all congregate, think and plan the next move.
Who knows, maybe he'll get around to finishing the house sometime.
Perce, played by the intense Monty Clift, is a young wanderer living on the dream of something more around the corner, risking injury to ride any horse at any cost.
Marilyn Monroe's portrayal of the sensuously beautiful, newly divorced Roslyn is fresh with emotion and distrust.
Her crusty seasoned girlfriend Isabelle, played by Thelma Ritter, is an authority on brokenness in marriage.

Been there and done that, many times.
She is loaded with battle scars, antidotes and a bottle.
The search for love, friendship and wholeness is unmasked when the three men plan to corral and round up some mustang horses to sell for dog food.
These scenes are compelling and riveting as the men work together to rope and bind a mare with her foal.
The stallion comes looking for them and then he is captured and bound.
Sensitive, skittish, horror-stricken Monroe fights vehemently to get these horses freed and she does.
"To play Roslyn, it is clear that Monroe (for whom Miller wrote the part) held up a mirror." (5)
All of the men were in love with her.
All were failures at some level.
Both women had been crushed by rejection.
The torture of the horses was a means to an end.
A few bucks for the day.
Everyone searches for fulfillment.
With great frustration, Guido summed up the void by articulating, "I can't remember how to land my plane and I can't find my way to God."
Lostness.
In one wrenching scene, Roslyn attempted an almost inaudible whisper; she looked up and voiced the word, "H E L P."
It was a cry in slow motion, a silent scream.
Exhaustion.
No plan.
No rest.
No answer.
No God.
Yes, we can identify with the movie.
We have lost our way to God.
We must stand up and seek.

"There are an infinity of angles at which one falls, only one at which one stands".
– G. K. Chesterton

God is not lost.

From the poem, *Where Are You*, we read these words:

"…I must reckon with you now, God
No longer cloud or fiery pillar;
No white-robed visitor in my tent,
And when I am afraid, it is hard to remember that Christ was alone and afraid
– except sometimes when someone reminds me.

Dear God,
How many people are there like me – and I have not reminded them?
Help me to bring Your loving presence – not cloud or fire – just by touching
another hand or making a phone call or smiling." (6)

Or writing in a book,
Or remembering a hymn.

On Christ the solid rock I stand,
All other ground is sinking sand.
All other ground is sinking sand.

I cannot stand on sand.
I need a Rock.

Stand at the crossroads and look....

God offers rest.
    "It's a unique form of rest. It's to rest in him in the midst of our threats
and burdens... God is our rock and our refuge right in the thick of our
situation."(7)
HE comes when we whisper, "H E L P!"

ARRESTING THOUGHTS

1.   When was the last time you looked at your life and questioned your
      direction?

2.   Why is it so hard to STOP?

3.   Does God have a plumb line, a measure from which we can get our
      bearings? Look up Amos 7:7-8

REST ASSURED

"Whenever anything begins to disintegrate your life in Jesus Christ, turn to Him at once and ask Him to establish rest."
– Oswald Chambers

A PILLOW PRAYER

Oh Lord;
I am so tired and spent from running on empty.
Activity has consumed my life.
I do not know how to stop but I must.
Most of my life I have felt like a misfit.
Then YOU came.
YOUR LOVE is the possibility that can continually fill up my life with hope.
I need YOUR Hand.
Show me the way to YOUR REST.
Come.
H E L P!
I repent.
Jesus I come to YOU.
Give me the assurance I can rest in YOU.
I know YOU are my Father and I am your child.
I love YOU.

Chapter Three

EXPLORING ANCIENT PATHS

To explore is to dig.
Faith examines.

It is a worthy fascination to study the lives of people who knew that God's requirements were not given as weights to burden them but as a means to exercise faith and yes, rest.
Abraham was such a man who understood the difference.
Our world is frantically searching for the latest self-help guru promising a formula that will instantly change our circumstance and bring respite.
Soon we realize there is no permanent way out of drivenness except to halt.
Men and women don't need to read another book,
But they need release, to be reminded of a rest found through a worthy obedience.

"Pride is heavy.
It weighs.
It is a fatness of spirit, an overindulgence of self.
This gluttony is earthbound,
Cannot be lifted up.
Help me to fast, to lose this weight!
Otherwise, O Light One,
How can I rejoice in your Ascension?" (1)

We must rediscover, go back to some ancient paths, and peruse the lives of men and women that followed God without a map, a workshop or a planner.
Abraham and Sarah, who began their lives as Abram and Sarai, were a patriarchal couple raised up for us to study as trailblazers.
They had foibles, frailty and fear, but also faith enough to believe God and to obey HIM.

Their journey taught them how to experience the "rest of God."
We can also.

Leave your country, your people and your father's household and go to the land I will
show you. (2)

God requires HIS followers to act, to risk, to obey.
He made a covenant with Abraham, a binding contract, an agreement.

I will make you a great nation and I will bless you and I will make your name great. (3)

This was the promise of God to Abraham but a whole lot of living had to come
before this reality was to be.
God keeps His word.

What do we know about Abraham?
Born near the city of Ur in the land known as Mesopotamia, he was one of
three sons. His father, Terah, was a worshipper of heathen gods. (4)
His brothers, Nahor and Haran, had flocks and herds.
It was a caravan life with tents that moved from place to place.
God called him to leave his "roots" and journey to an unknown land at age
seventy five.
It must have seemed untimely to uproot his wife Sarah, but he did.
Together with his nephew, Lot, they gathered up all their possessions and
attempted to begin again in the land of Canaan.
Why?
Because that is what God wanted him to do.
How?

By faith Abraham, when called to go to a place he would later receive as his inheritance,
obeyed and went, even though he did not know where he was going.... By faith he
made his home in the Promised Land like a stranger in a foreign country; he lived in
tents as did Issac and Jacob, who were heirs with him of the same promise. (5)

Pick up and go.
Live in a tent.
Take your livestock.
Bring your family.

The Lord appeared to him and said, "To your offspring I will give this land." So he built an altar there to the Lord who had appeared to him. (6)

Wherever he pitched his tent, he also built an altar.
Building an altar was a practice to cause the people to pause and thank God for provision, honoring HIS guidance.
This would be a forerunner of keeping the Sabbath.
Worship would become an integral part of life.
It was needed as a reminder of God's Grace
But there were more moves ahead.
From Shechem towards Negeb, Egypt to Bethel, Abraham traveled with his family, finally settling in Mamre near Hebron.
Drought and famine drove him to Egypt.
A lack of trust in God's continuous endowment and fear for personal safety caused him to misrepresent Sarah as his sister to Pharaoh.

I know what a beautiful woman you are. When the Egyptians see you, they will say, "This is his wife." Then they will kill me but will let you live. Say you are my sister, so I will be treated well for your sake and my life will be spared because of you. (7)

How preposterous this was for a husband to intentionally put his beloved wife up for compromise because he was afraid.
But he did and Sarah agreed.
Deception and opportunism began to surface.
This couple had flaws.
Sarah was, indeed, very beautiful and was taken into the palace.
As a result, Abraham's wealth increased as sheep, cattle, male and female donkeys, men and maid servants and even camels were acquired.
What a scenario.
It appears that Sarah was used for a means to and end, hustled by her own husband for personal gain.
Trumped up schemes of greed and covetousness do not work.
How easily we seem to distort the ways of God.
Pharaoh became disturbed over an outbreak of serious diseases inflicted upon his household. He felt it was a directive from God as a consequence of Abraham's willful deception concerning Sarah.
Questioned by Pharaoh, caught in a lie, Abraham hit the road again with his wife and entourage.
Going to Negeb, he became wealthy again and his livestock, silver and gold increased.

Trouble, however, began to erupt between the herdsmen of Abraham and his nephew Lot, and they decided to separate.

Lot chose the plains of Jordan and Abraham chose Canaan.

Once again the God of the universe spoke to Abraham and said, *"Lift up your eyes from where you are and look north and south, east and west. All the land you see I will give to you and your offspring forever. I will make your offspring like the dust of the earth.... Go, walk through the length and the breadth of the land for I am giving it to you."* (8)

This was the promise of God to Abraham as he learned to walk the land in faith, a reminder of His covenant.

There were threatening battles awaiting Abraham.

He rescued Lot with 318 men.

He returned a tithe from the spoils unto Melchizedek, King of Salem.

He wrestled with the barrenness of Sarah,

BUT...

Abraham believed the Lord and he credited it to Him as righteousness. (9)

Age was advancing upon Abraham and Sarah.

Men manipulate and so do women.

No child had been born to Sarah and biologically, it seemed impossible.

After living in Canaan for ten years, she came up with plan B.

Her name was Hagar, an Egyptian maidservant.

Sarah decided to give her to Abraham in order to conceive a child.

It happened.

Jealousy entered.

Women compete.

Whose fault was it?

A mistreated, impregnated Hagar flees to the desert where an angel of the Lord appears to her beside a spring and says to her, *"You are now with child and you shall have a son. You shall name him Ishmael for the Lord has heard your misery."* (10)

Hagar responds, *"You are the God who sees me...I have now seen the One who sees me."* (11)

Ishmael was not the promised seed of Abraham but Almighty God heard the cries of an outcast, pregnant young woman and made purveyance for her.

HE still comes to the destitute and delivers compassion.

Ishmael was born to Abraham at the age of 86.

Thirteen years later at age 99, God comes to Abraham once again and confirms his covenant to "greatly increase your numbers."

God keeps His Word.
At this juncture, the name *Abram* is changed officially to Abraham and he is called the "father of many nations."
Sarai becomes Sarah and is told she will have a son.
Abraham laughs.
Then Sarah laughs.

Is anything too hard for the Lord? (12)

Oh the impossibilities of life which are not so for God!
Once again, this nomadic couple went on the road but this time they traveled into the region of Negev, staying in Gerar.
One more time, Sarah is pawned off as his sister to King Abimelech.
Repeatedly Abraham is confronted for his seemingly persistent deception.
God intervenes on Sarah's behalf,
But a tiny insight emerges in scripture which sheds light upon this awkward subterfuge between Sarah and Abraham.

…She really is my sister, the daughter of my father, though not of my mother; and she became my wife. And when God had me wander from my father's household, I said to her, this is how you can show your love to me: Everywhere we go, say of me, "He is my brother." (13)

We do not know all things.
Sarah and Abraham had agreed that this marital caveat would be an expression of love, demonstrated as needed.
It was a pact.
For better or worse
Richer or poorer
In sickness and in health
As man and wife or
As brother and sister.
What seemed a travesty was a test of faith and loyalty to one another.
They were committed to each other.
They rested in this arrangement.
God was committed to them.
Sarah conceived.
Isaac was born.
The promises of God prove true.
God keeps His word.

There would be other tests for Abraham, other altars, other opportunities to choose to follow God's commands.

He would have to cast Ishmael from his home as a boy to preserve the peace with Sarah, but according to scripture, God provided for this son.

Take him by the hand for I will make him into a great nation.
God was with the boy as he grew up.
He lived in the desert and became an archer. (14)

The Lord provided for Ishmael.

Later on Abraham would be asked to take Isaac, the son of promise, up to a mountain in Moriah and place him on an altar prepared for a sacrifice.

In obedience Abraham is found again at a crossroads of faith.

Imagine this father's anguished heart.

This was a witness of the will.

When Isaac questioned his father as to where the lamb was for the sacrifice, Abraham answered, "*God Himself will provide the burnt offering, my son.*" (15)

Indeed HE did.

Miraculously God mediates.

Do not lay a hand on the boy…Now I know that you fear God because you have not withheld from me your son… (16)

Abraham had learned to rest in the promises of God.

The quest for rest will involve tests.

We now, in retrospect, glean the guiding mandates of God upon his life.

Believe, obey, follow, worship and then rest in me.

Yes, he missed the mark many times and so will we.

Following after God will involve a surrendered allegiance but following fuels faith, sustains and trains, redefines and renews us.

Because it is God's "doing" there will be balance, and where there is balance there is rest, a God-ordained center from which one can operate.

Abraham and Sarah were not perfect.

In fact they were as blemished as we.

On occasion they attempted to recreate their destiny and failed,

So do we.

Ishmael was born to Hagar, plan B.

Isaac was born to Sarah, plan A.

In old age there was fulfillment of plan A.

Both births were known by God.

Neither was beyond His reach.
Only one was the chosen seed.
Self-help almost wrecked their lives.
God was trying to establish within them deference and dependence.
HE is still trying to do this with us.
"They crossed deserts, rode camels, acquired wealth, suffered childlessness, sacrificed much, received promises, and caught a glimpse of the Glory of God." (17)
We have strayed far away from the ancient paths.
We have substituted our own plans for God's ways.
In cities, towns and deserts, altars were constructed to help the people remember God.
We build altars for ourselves in order to catch up, sleep in, play up, vegetate, let down.
We are exhausted and spent because we have forgotten HIM.
Even in calamity and confusion, with schemes and diversions, Abraham and Sarah knew the justice and the reward in obeying God.
His plans succeed.
Sometimes they could not see or imagine how.
They walked by faith.
Through failure they returned to the proven path
And so must we.
His mercy is momentously crucial.
We must return to some ancient paths.

Remember this, fix it in mind, take it to heart, you rebels.
Remember the former things, those of long ago;
I am God, and there is no other;
I am God, and there is none like me.
I make known the end from the beginning, from ancient times, what is still to come, I say: My purpose will stand.... What I have said that will I bring about; what I have planned, that I will do. (18)

God's precepts bring rest....
The worship of God strengthens us from within.
His rest is more than a scheduled slot on the day-timer or a reminder on the Blackberry.
We must come back to the core values found in the Bible.
The Lord will provide.

I sing because I'm happy.
I sing because I'm free.
His eye is on the sparrow for I know he cares for me.

When I can sing, I know HE is ahead of me, orchestrating my way.
When I can sing about His Love, I am free.
When I can sing, I know His rest.

The ancient paths worked.
"These ancient stories are our stories. These stories are reflective of how things are."(19)
They are a reality check of our present day culture.
"What we want is relief. We want our problem or heartache to just go away. And yet the message of biblical rest is that your relief may come from the power you gain when you accept your suffering. Your relief may come from the strength you develop from serving in spite of it." (20)

Those who feared the Lord spoke to one another,
And the Lord listened and heard them;
So a book of remembrance was written before Him for those who fear the Lord and who meditate on His Name. (21)

Remember.
Return.
Rest.
The Lord will provide.

ARRESTING THOUGHTS

1.   How do you define obedience?

2.   What happens when we run away from God?

3.   What can we learn from the life of Abraham and Sarah that will promote our returning to a path of faith?

REST ASSURED

"Conviction, were it never so excellent, is worthless till it converts itself into Conduct."
– Thomas Carlyle

A PILLOW PRAYER

Holy Father;
I see more clearly now why I do not experience YOUR rest.
I have attempted to live life on the terms I create.
I understand now that feelings have nothing to do with obedience for obedience is an act of my will.
I can choose to obey YOU.
I identify with the void of worship.
The altar of me is exhausting.
Help me, Lord to change.
I bow down and ask forgiveness for running down the path of false reward.
I must turn around and run to YOU, Sovereign King.
YOU bring perspective and rest.
New habits I must learn.
By grace, YOU will guide me.
By faith, I will seek after YOU.
By Love I shall live unto YOUR WAYS, O Ancient of Days.
Because of JESUS, I can return.

Chapter Four

RECLAIMING TRUST

Trust must be found.
Faith waits.

I love Sunday mornings.
To anticipate the experience of being in corporate worship and to hear the Word of God proclaimed fills up a deep yearning within me.
It is a part of my week I look forward to with gladness.
I enjoy the quietness found in the early morning.
To me it is a gift.
I always expect to bring home a word from God I will need to integrate into my life.
I awakened one particular spring Sunday morning to pleasant, cloudless skies and immediately opened the patio door and turned on the outside fountain.
It is a comforting sound.
The trickling of the water is like a musical interlude inviting me to begin the day with thanksgiving to my Heavenly Father.
My clothing had been laid out the night before.
My time in prayer had been energizing and after eating a small bowl of oatmeal at the breakfast table, I prepared to take my vitamins.
Every evening I place my jewelry in a small box which has a lid. The box rests in a tray on the counter top near my refrigerator in an area of daily activity.
This morning I had taken out my wedding rings and cleaned them, placing them back into the box with my watch, a scripture bracelet and my favorite tiny silver "knot" earrings. Everything in this collection I wear every day.
They are my uniform in adornment.
In my multi-tasking in the kitchen, wiping the counter tops, making coffee, I must have swept up an ear ring by mistake in my hand and inadvertently dropped it into the vitamin bowl.
How?
I do not know?
But that's what had happened.

Grabbing a handful of vitamins in the right hand, and holding a glass of water in my left hand, I gulped them down.

There seemed to be a bit of a catch in my throat.

The instant I swallowed I knew one of those "knot" earrings was gone.

It is so odd.

I just knew.

Before I went to confirm it, I realized I must drink another whole glass of water quickly to ensure the passage of this object.

It cleared and then fear began its work.

I rushed to the box of jewelry and sure enough one earring was gone.

I stood for a few moments in utter disbelief.

I did swallow a quarter as a kid, but how could a reasonably sane adult swallow an earring?

I did say "reasonably."

Questions began to bombard me.

What must I do next?

Do I wake up Roy?

Should I call a doctor?

Do I need to go into the emergency room at the hospital?

First things first, right?

I woke up Roy and explained what had happened.

He kept asking me if I were sure that I had actually done this.

And I kept saying, "Yes, I am sure."

Then he suggested I call the doctor, which I did. The doctor said very calmly to me, "If it has cleared your esophagus, then it will pass through your body in about three days. There is nothing to do but wait."

I breathed in a sigh of doomed acceptance.

What goes in comes out.

This reality hit me with a grateful but guarded resolve.

What next?

I did not feel sick.

Was I going to lie down for three days, eat lightly, and drink tons of liquids?

What was I to do?

I just felt like someone who had entered a time warp, a serious rite of passage that would require God's intervention.

At the back of the earring was a sharp silver post which was shielded by a flat rubber earring back.

As long as this plastic back was attached to the post, there was safety.

If it came off, then the danger of perforating the stomach or intestinal tract was real.

So I knew I was to pray for God's protection and to ask a few trusted friends to do so as well.

With this prayer pact in place, I dressed and went to church deciding that now I was in the midst of an adventure of trust and a unique opportunity to demonstrate my faith through praise.

...If anyone serves he should do it with the strength God provides, that in all things God may be praised in Jesus Christ.... (1)

In all things, Lord?
The Word of God says, "In all things."
Oh, how the power of praise breaks anxiety, dispels panic and causes us to believe God is able.
I put on a choir robe and opened up my heart to sing of the God who gives us peace as we trust in HIM in unusual circumstances.
I experienced a worship of the will.

Come, let us sing for joy to the Lord.... Let us come before him with thanksgiving and extol him with music and song. (2)

As I sang, I imagined the earring tunneling through the channels of my body.
I prayed, "Heavenly Father, accept my praise."

"A soul redeemed demands a life of praise."
William Cowper

My heart had to flow unto Him.
It was a day of creative grace that I shall not soon forget.
I had to choose to trust God or succumb to a quaking dread.
The next two days progressed with a watchful eye and an assuring trust.
Apprehension passed.
So did the earring.

But in your hearts set apart Christ as Lord. Always be prepared to give an answer to everyone who asks you to give the reason for the hope you have. (3)

Sometimes the trust God wants us to reclaim will require much more effort than a bizarre earring dilemma.
"A personal crisis is creative and salutary if one can accept the conflict and restore unity on a higher level." (4)
We already know we cannot control what happens to us but we can choose to make our God Lord over all.

While traveling with my husband, Roy, to the New Orleans area last summer to speak, we were carefully reading our directions to the home of Betsy and Bob, our hosts.

As we searched for the correct number, I noticed a sign in the yard of what appeared to be our hosts' home. The sign read, "Jesus is Lord of all."

We learned that this was the home this dear couple had found to lease after theirs was destroyed in Hurricane Katrina.

The owner was a dentist.

He had chosen to have about fifty of these signs printed and strategically placed on his properties as well as his dental offices. He also gave them to members of his church congregation.

Betsy had been praying about finding a house for them to rent. Driving up to this property she saw this sign and knew it was the place God had chosen for them.

Since 1976, she told me they had chosen to live out God's plan for them whatever it might be, surrendering all control unto Him.

Betsy is a cancer survivor, an intercessor, a sister in Christ Jesus.

She had discovered a trust in HIM that did not need reclaiming for it was alive and well. Life can scatter us.

The secure cannot be scattered.

Therefore my heart is glad and my tongue rejoices; my body also will rest secure. (5)

We can throw trust out the window because of feelings of outrage at our bad fortune or we can "turn every thought that would lead ill will into prayer." (6) Conscious premeditated praise will bring us into security every time.

If we do not, we shall be carried away into the rush of the unpredictable and soon our trust will have to be reclaimed because it is buried in despair.

Swallowing, wallowing, singing or wringing, one day, "At the name of Jesus every knee shall bow in heaven and on earth and under the earth and every tongue will confess that Jesus Christ is Lord." (7)

"Only those who really know how to worship can really enjoy His rest." (8) So sing to the Lord in trouble.

Bring HIM praise.

All to Jesus I surrender.
All to Him I freely give
I will ever love and trust Him.
In His presence daily live.

He will be the Lord over all then.
Why not make HIM Lord over all now?
If we do, we can know a trust that rests in the midst of frightful alarm for praise to the God of all Gods; the King of all Kings breaks, interrupts and dispels any foreboding.
I know.
HE is LORD.

ARRESTING THOUGHTS

1. When crisis strikes, why do we tend to turn to everyone else but God?

2. Can we find rest (assurance) in calamity, based on Philippians 4:11-13?

3. What does it mean to acknowledge Jesus as Lord over all?

REST ASSURED

"Let nothing disturb thee;
Let nothing disturb thee;
All things pass
God never changes."
– St. Teresa de Cepeda

A Pillow Prayer

Holy Father;
I know YOU are there beside me when I am in trouble, when I am afraid, when I try to reason out the next move.
When did I detour from belief into disbelief?
What caused me to strike out on my own and to begin to live without faith in

YOU?

Why am I so scattered when difficulty comes?

I repent.

I have veered away from YOUR RESOURCES.

Call me back.

Forgive my wandering heart.

I will drive down a stake today in the confidence found in YOU ALONE.

I will believe YOU can do the impossible when it arrives.

In fact, I will declare it.

Praise YOU for every circumstance that comes my way causing me to seize upon YOUR empowering TRUST.

Reclaimed, I can now find my way through and once again rest in YOU.

In Jesus' Name, I come.

Chapter Five

THE GOOD WAY

God is good.
Faith must act.

I fell asleep with the cognizance that I must awaken early the next morning to prepare for my flight to Ohio.

It was not a predawn rising but since my body, mind and spirit had been stretched way beyond the norm for even a high energy person like me, I needed extra time to prepare.

My husband, Roy, and I had unloaded and flattened 52 moving boxes the day before.

While my 81 year old mother was recovering from a broken pelvic bone in a Rehab hospital and my 81 year old stepfather was in his weekly dialysis, we were receiving and unpacking the household goods at their new retirement patio home which is about five minutes from us. The former home had been sold and closed.

Roy analyzes and executes.

I organize and create.

We are a seasoned team with thirty years of experience in moving with the Navy.

We both can visualize with imagination something beautiful from brown cardboard boxes.

It is the making of a home…a place of refuge, sanctuary, a place of rest.

We knew Mother and Hugh would love this "resting place" as they began to walk through their ninth decade and fourth year of marriage.

Living life requires change, reorientation and time.

The toll of this three-day whirlwind of activity for me was an aching body, a bedraggled mind and a heart that needed resuscitating.

I was depleted.

Thinking about going into six degree weather on Lake Erie at a retreat center required packing warm clothing, which takes up more suitcase space, creating more to do.

My whole being cried out for divine traction, a suspension to stretch the tension of my muscles and unburden my soul at the same time.

Upon arriving at the airport, within minutes, I was informed that my flight was cancelled.

This was not what I expected.

I was then rescheduled to leave in the early afternoon, so I had four and one half hours to spend at the airport.

My immediate reaction, as everyone else's, was, "Oh Lord, one more adversity!"

After speaking to Roy, I pondered going back home but decided to stay at the airport.

"Lord, the delay is YOUR doing. Now, what is YOUR plan for the day, what is YOUR way?"

The direction slowly began to expand.

First things first.

I was hungry, so I ate a muffin.

I made some important telephone calls concerning mother's healthcare crisis and the finalizing of some details concerning this ongoing move, which was to happen in a couple of weeks.

I checked in with my mother and my daughter.

Then I wrote two notes to two new acquaintances in my church, one in grief and one beginning her journey with cancer.

Next I felt compelled to call three other close friends, my hostess Nita who was to pick me up in Akron so she would know the change in arrival time, and Peggy and Beth who pray me through all I do.

More connecting.

And then I was very deliberately led to the Word of God.

Today it was the book of Lamentations.

I was lamenting,

So was Jeremiah.

He described a loving, faithful God who took time to warn a rebellious people over and over again of the consequences of disobedience, a people who would not stop long enough to hear truth.

It was the familiar story of knowing "the good way" but rejecting it.

Sovereign God had allowed Jerusalem to be taken into captivity by the Babylonians. His people had turned from following HIM and embraced idolatry. Their hearts were hardened and unrepentant. It is the unveiling of a grieving God and the reality that because of Jerusalem's sin, "she finds no resting place." (1)

Exile, affliction, wandering, abandonment are all consequences for wrong choices.

Sin cannot be tolerated by a holy God.
There were cries for consolation.
I absorbed the smothering helplessness.

...the Lord has sapped my strength. (2)

Then confession comes.

The Lord is righteous, yet I rebelled against His command. (3)

His broken heart is revealed.

...my heart is poured out on the ground because my people are destroyed. (4)

Our God is wounded when we rebel.
The gravity of distancing ourselves from God is found in these words: "no relief, no rest."
In this state of separation HE cautions His people to "*...arise, cry out in the night as the watches of the night begin; pour out your heart like water in the presence of the Lord. Lift up your hands to Him for the lives of your children.*" (5)

The judgment of God is now upon His beloved Jerusalem.

The Lord has done what he planned; he has fulfilled his word, which he decreed long ago. He has overthrown you without pity, he has let the enemy gloat over you, he has exalted the horn of your foes. (6)

The enemy was allowed to overcome.
God had done this but in the midst of this crisis, His great love broke the barrier.
It always does.

Because of the LORD's great love we are not consumed, for his compassions never fail. They are new every morning; great is your faithfulness. (7)

HE is faithful.
HE waits for us to turn back.

You, O LORD, reign forever; your throne endures from generation to generation... Restore us to yourself, O Lord, that we may return; renew our days as of old.... (8)

Deliverance is promised if we turn back.
What a pattern given to His own.
Repent and be restored.
We have a Savior who is always ready to rendezvous with us.
Today the clock had stopped for me.
For four hours I had been encapsulated.
Kairos time.
God and me.
The promises of God laced with caution and love had made me so aware of His all knowing sagacious perspective.
It was personal instruction for me.
I drank from the well of the Word and was rejuvenated completely.
My original plan for this airport time was to land somewhere with my travel pillow and roll up for a few hours to catch up on rest.
That did not happen.
Instead I ate because I was hungry.
I reconnected with my Creator.
I studied a Biblical letter of parental warning and consequence.
I was given time to receive and the exhausted empty place inside me was filled.
This study in God's Word is a reflection of our present day spiritual rebellion.
People have ceased to think on God.
They have substituted many things but none satisfies.
Yes, idols are still with us.
They aren't always graven images.
Sometimes they are images we integrate into our lives.
The search for meaning abounds.
Statistics are brutally graphic.
"In 2002 about 18 million adults in the United States met the diagnostic criteria for alcohol disorders." (9)

"An estimated 1.8 million of youth age twelve and older are current users of cocaine." (10)

"In children who are diagnosed with Type II diabetes, 85% are obese." (11)

"Thirty eight per cent of adults believe it is 'morally acceptable' to look at pictures
involving explicit sexual behavior." (12)

"Seventy per cent of female inmates in American prisons were initially arrested for prostitution." (13)

Our attempts to satisfy the God void within us are failing.
Alcohol, drugs, food and sexual cravings are just a few of the appetites which have caused us to veer off course from the "good way."
We are dying for lack of purpose.

"They made their own traditions God."
Alfred Lord Tennyson

We are crying out for someone to stop the pain.
We continue down the road that leads to nowhere.
We must stop, turn around and seek God once again.

I am the Lord your God,
Who teaches you what is best for you,
Who directs you in the way you should go. (14)

He has never left us.
As I stood up strengthened from my encounter with God's presence through His Word, I realized that four and one half hours had vanished into my soul and I was now ready to "go and do" because I had been captivated, challenged, and recharged to live and embrace the "the good way."
As I boarded the plane, I found my seat and began to settle in when I observed a snapshot of the restlessness that our over achieving, driven society portrays. An attractive, slender, disheveled blonde about thirty was struggling to get down the aisle. She was completely laden down with a brown bag bulging with papers on one shoulder and a computer on the other. To add to her balancing act, a black, rolling suitcase was trailing behind. Her layered bangs revealed an intelligent, but tired face that was desperately trying to exude confidence as a cell phone was encapsulated between the right cheek of her face and the crook of her neck. While maneuvering the cart and looking for her seat, she never missed a beat in her conversation on the phone. Finally there was a slowing down in the line of travelers progressing toward their seats and everyone close by heard her conversation.
"Yes, how are you? Great. How are things going down there? Really, well I am boarding a plane right now...could you send me an e-mail? Oh, will you be in Atlanta next week? Where is your meeting? OK...could we meet then for breakfast or lunch? (By now the line had begun to move) Yes, I can. I

will put the info into my palm pilot. Super. Thanks." Not once did she miss a word of conversation as the cell phone remained precariously in place. At last she edged into her seat across from me with the final words to her contact, "Thanks." Immediately she dumped the computer and shoulder bags down on her seat and then placed them under the seat in front. The rolling cart went onto the overhead. I turned away to get a book out of my tote bag and glanced over at her. She had collapsed into her "temporary resting place" and instantly her eyes were closed.

Cell phones dominate the days of our lives.

Cell phones do not create time.

They decimate it.

Cell phone faith won't provide the rest we need.

To close the deal of living every day, we must meet with God.

There must be rest...a rest that is not just a number, a dial tone, a program of minutes or a package of perks designed to give lots of extras.

HE is rest.

HE is a good God.

There is a good way.

Goodness is one of his attributes but there is more.

Behold the goodness and severity of God. (15)

Give thanks unto the Lord, for he is good. (16)

"Either God is good and in control or it all depends on you."(17)

In Psalm 107, we read about the cries of His children and His action for them.

...for he satisfies the thirsty and fills the hungry with good things... Then they cried to the Lord in their trouble and he saved them from their distress. (18)

Behold His goodness.

HE is holy and just.

But they had rebelled against the Word of God and despised the counsel of the Most High so he subjected them to bitter labor; they stumbled and there was no one to help. (19)

Behold His severity.

Whoever is wise let him heed these things and consider the great love of the Lord. (20)

We are to "appreciate the goodness of God…. Calvary is the measure of the goodness of God; lay it to heart. Ask yourself the psalmist's question – 'What shall I render unto the LORD for all his benefits toward me?' Appreciate the patience of God. Think how he has borne with you, and still bears with you…. Learn to marvel at His patience and seek grace to imitate it…. Appreciate the discipline of God…all things come of Him and you have tasted his goodness every day of your life. If He puts thorns in your bed, it is only to awaken you…to make you rise up and seek his mercy…to ensure that you continue in his goodness by letting your sense of need bring you back constantly in…faith to seek his face. This kindly discipline in which God's severity touches us for a moment…is a discipline of love." (21)

Goodness and severity mark the good way.

It seems paradoxical.

"We can find the good life only when we understand we aren't good." (22).

Evil exists but so does the goodness of God.

We have the power to choose the good way.

My breakpoint in the airport with God was a precious pause, a "pillow time" with God.

Now I could see more clearly what surrounded me.

God has plans for us each day in every circumstance.

When we deviate into our own, we lose the good way.

The Word of God had halted my fatigue, refreshed my soul and cradled my expectations with hope.

I was restored.

How?

Physical exhaustion.

A cancelled flight.

Time tethered with the Savior.

Weaned from weariness.

Buoyed to continue.

Invigorated by His incredible Love.

Multiplied minutes.

I found my pillow, my resting place.

The Good Way works.

Upon my arrival at Lake Erie, it was completely frozen and it seemed as though piles of snow randomly zig zagged all across the lake in strange lines.

This was a busy camp with retreats for all ages and stages of life.

When I met the camp director after settling in a bit, I asked him about the intriguing design of the snow.

He smiled and said, "No snow games, Mrs. Cash, those were waves that froze."
Frozen waves?
White snow ruffles welcomed me to a weekend in God's Word.
I rarely see snow.
"It snows only once in our dreams." (23)
But it was to be a snowbound encapsulating time around the warmth found in God's Word.
I was so refreshed and ready.
Fatigue robs us of wonder.
Rest reveals it.
My heart sang these words:

God is so good
God is so good.
God is so good.
He's so good to me
And you.

ARRESTING THOUGHTS

1. Do you recognize disruptions in your life as God's restraint?

2. How can we train our hearts to redeem time for God?

3. Is it your habit to carry a Bible with you wherever you go?

REST ASSURED

"Only the hand that erases can write the true thing."
– Meister Eckhart

A PILLOW PRAYER

God of all time;
I come.
Today, bogged down with my own worn out baggage, I stopped to open up YOUR world in the Word.
Out there on my own, I had stuffed my suitcases with pity and blame.
Seeking after YOU, I unpacked anxiety, released fatigue and was given a fresh supply of grace to wear.
YOUR mercies are new every morning.
I had forgotten.
Today I experienced YOUR REST.
How beautiful is YOUR compassionate Love for us.
Always waiting for us to look up and find YOU were there all the time waiting for our fellowship.
YOU mean good for us.
YOUR WAY is good.
Forgive our rebellion, sloth, apathy.
Be our pillow even in an airport.
In Jesus' Name, we rest.

Chapter Six

REVIVING RELEVANCE

The Bible is relevant.
Faith testifies.

At some point in the quest for rest, we are drawn into someone's story which tests the premise of Biblical relevance.
How do people overcome?
What is the way?
Whom did they lean on?
Is faith relevant?
Are we?
Pray tell, what is relevant?
Throughout centuries of pursuing God, men and women have laid hold of truths found in the Bible.
Why?
Because it is relevant, current, apropos, timely, seasonable, opportunely on the cutting edge of criticism, cause, clarity and confidence.
It will show us how to get to the crux, the solution: the path to God.
It interrupts the crisis-driven courtrooms of the mind where reason and logic have long been abandoned and where the emotional dramas of our society are played out in themes of "how I feel." It blows holes in our warring for significance because it positions God's peace as a sentinel at the gate of our lives.
Where HE guards the gate there is hope.
The Bible documents the lives of real people who lived sometimes exclusively unto themselves, achieved and over-achieved and then became worn out and prostrate by life.
Sounds like us, don't you think?
The gate to Him was accessible then.
It still is.
But we fail to open it.
We matter to God.
We must because Jesus came for us.

Therefore we must also be relevant.
Solomon was just such a man, a man searching for relevance.
The book of Ecclesiastes launches the search for a meaningful life.

What is twisted cannot be straightened; what is lacking cannot be counted. (1)

If this is true, why bother?

Does the pursuit of wisdom work?

For with much wisdom comes much sorrow;
The more knowledge the more grief. (2)

Are we accountable for what we do with what we have?

What about pleasure?

I denied myself nothing my eyes desired.
I refused my heart no pleasure. (3)

Solomon amassed silver, gold, vineyards, gardens, reservoirs, men and women singers to entertain and a harem of many wives, but he still agonized over his lack of fulfillment.
What about work?

> *For a man may do his work with wisdom, knowledge and skill, and then he must leave all he owns to someone who has not worked for it. This, too, is meaningless.* (4)

He continues to bemoan the fruitless, vain, pointless future.
All is futile.
By our world's standard, Solomon had it all; but in his mind, life was a commiseration about the inadequacies, the injustices he observed.
He wanted to hold on to all.
One never can.
His diatribe about disappointment in life finally stacks up chapter by chapter until at last the breadth of God's reality crashes in "...*the righteous and the wise and what they do are in God's hands.*" (5)
Whose hands?
God's Hands.

So we are not alone.

The quiet words of the wise are more to be heeded than the shouts of fools. (6)

Wise words are a gift.

The heart of the wise inclines to the right. (7)

There is a sense of "rightness, fairness" to a wise man's ways.

Calmness can lay great errors to rest. (8)

Attitude matters.
These words came from the Bible.
Solomon struggled, pondered and debated his choices.
Subsequently he closes out this book surrendering to what is truly relevant.

Now all has been heard; here is the conclusion of the matter:
Fear God and keep his commandments, for this is the whole duty of man. (9)

How true.
How simple.
How completely profound.
A sweeping Truth found in the Word of God is the pillow upon which to lay our head.
Gaining and losing, striving and conniving, getting and giving, pleasuring and pining, spending and accruing, attaining and feigning are all pieces of the quest for a life of meaning. God gives us accounts of people who did it their way and failed.
And so do we.
Resting our lives under the preeminence of our Heavenly Father and keeping His commandments is what makes our lives relevant, pertinent, purposeful.
This is not a new concept but an old one that needs to be revitalized.
Why?
Because we need reviving.
The Bible repeats itself because we need to hear and appropriate its truth, again and again, and again!

The law of the Lord is perfect reviving the soul. (10)

The Bible revives.

Will you not revive us again? (11)

God is in the business of bringing us back to life lived in Him.
The cry for relevance is a cry for meaning.
We have criminals who are imprisoned because they blame society for not giving them what they want.
We have children whose childhoods have been taken away by irresponsible men and women living out bizarre and unnatural behavior.
We have a people who have railed against God because of disaster, financial set backs or illness.
How does the Word of God speak to us today as we attempt to survive a culture that is "all about me"?

It was the summer of 2005 when I met Jan.
Instantly we were sisters in faith and fellowship.
Her life was a vivacious, expressive, passionate, fountain pouring out for others.
Her smile was a contagious expletive.
Her countenance reflected the beauty of Christ born in her heart and lived out with a magnetic love.
She drew people to Jesus just by her presence.
I was one of them.
Hear these words written by Jan as she entered into a life altering experience with God in the furnace of affliction.

For the word of God is living and active (12)

"For years I have been in various Bible studies, guided Bible Coffees and taught in-depth Biblical faith-based lessons to women of all ages. Yet it wasn't until 2006 that I became truly aware of the realness and intimacy of God's Word being initiated and applied to my very own life...changing me forever...which is where HE wanted to take me all along...in His Presence. That was the year I was diagnosed with cancer...twice. That was also the year God led me to understand that the 'Big C' stands for Christ. While enduring a grueling round of six weeks of radiation to my neck and head region, God's Word always accompanied me. Literally, I placed a Bible under my legs during the daily treatments, yet spiritually God's Word was brought forth through my mind and heart with visuals. As the technicians would assist me onto the therapy table...I

was being laid upon an altar. With each treatment my hands were even bound. The actual radiation machine became the Refiner's Fire.... The story of Isaac became my visual. Although I had been asked to surrender myself fully to the altar, I went willingly, knowing my Jesus had already gone to the cross for me as my substitute. This was just a test...of whether or not I would trust God in His Word. With each radiation treatment, a mask had to be snapped down all around my head so that its placement would be secure. Each time this tightly fitting mesh was placed on my face, I would close my eyes and meditate.... 'I am now wearing the helmet of my salvation.' God's Word would always come forth and specific passages would visually become active and clear. Reciting II Chronicles 20 became alive for me.... Each day I 'marched down, stood firm and took my position to see the deliverance of the Lord.'
AND HE DELIVERED ME.

Six months later I found myself back in God's battlefield as I entered the breast cancer clinic to be prepped for a lumpectomy. I had been informed that lymph nodes, referred to as your sentinel nodes (Gatekeepers) would be removed during this procedure as a precautionary measure to check for any invasiveness of the cancer. Immediately I was intrigued by the terminology of the 'Gatekeepers.' While waiting for pre-op, with Bible in hand, God's Spirit led me to a passage in I Chronicles 9. I became in awe of God's Word as I continued to read and began to recognize what He was showing me. 'Gatekeepers' were put in place to guard God's temple. Hundreds guarded the various thresholds altogether, but what significantly spoke to me was the 'Gatekeepers' that guarded the FOUR main entrances to the temple (v.24) The 'Gatekeepers' were on all four sides representing the east, west, north and south. It was then that I closed my eyes claiming this Word as Truth for my life and I prayed, 'Dearest Lord Jesus, my body is your temple. Thank you that you reign over me and that you are with me now and will never leave me or forsake me. I ask that you surround your Gatekeepers over my breast – one at the north, south, east and west. I claim this Word as Truth I have received.' Amen.

Prior to my procedure, my surgeon informed me that every one has a different number of sentinel nodes so she would have no idea how many she would be removing until the operation. The anesthesia took effect while my husband was praying over me. As I awakened, my first question was, 'how many Gatekeepers did I have?'
My husband's reply ..., 'FOUR...AND THEY WERE ALL CLEAN.'"

He set forth his word and healed them. (13)

"God has brought forth a new presence of His Word to me. Every night I claim

scripture with 'expectancy', knowing it holds Resurrection Power!"
Then Jan listed these scriptures on which she stood in prayer.

You may ask for anything in my name and I will do it. (14)

If you remain in me and my words remain in you, ask whatever you wish and it will be given to you. (15)

Ask and it shall be given to you, seek and you will find; knock and the door will opened to you. (16)

Whatever you ask for in prayer; believe you have received it, and it will be yours. (17)

All things are possible to him who believes. (18)

Now faith is being sure of what we hope for, certain of what we do not see. (19)

For the Lord your God is the one who goes with you to fight for you against your enemies to give you victory. (20)

Jan concludes with these words, "MY LIFE IS NOW RESTING ON THE WORD OF GOD!"

The Bible is relevant.
"The word of God has to anchor itself in the center of our being. The art of spiritual living is to eat the word, digest it, and incorporate it concretely into our lives." (21)
Knowing and applying it brings a quiet confidence in the Living Lord.
Solomon was right.
Fear God and keep His commandments.
Faith grows when we observe someone "enhanced in every way by his relationship to God." (22)
A life of meaning rests on the pillow of God's Word.
Who is guarding your gates?
Know the sentinels.
You have them and so do I.
"Revive us once again, Lord."
The music of this refrain engages my heart:

Standing on the promises of Christ my King.
Through eternal ages let His praises ring.
Glory to the highest I will shout and sing, 'Standing on the promises of God'
Standing, standing,
Standing on the promise of God my Savior.
Standing, standing,
I'm standing on the promises of God.

When I am standing on the promises of God, I am at rest.

ARRESTING THOUGHTS

1.   In what ways can you identify with the "meaningless" mindset of Solomon?

2.   Do you have a reverential respect for God and His commandments? If not, why not?

3.   Could you face a devastating calamity like Jan's armed with the assurances found in God's Word?

REST ASSURED

"Nothing Before, Nothing Behind:
The steps of faith fall on the Seeming Void
And find the Rock Beneath."
– John Greenleaf Whittier

A PILLOW PRAYER

Holy Father;
Seeker of my heart, I present myself to YOU in confession.
I know YOUR WORD is Truth but I have not lived in it.
I have not lingered over its reality and learned to claim it for my own.
I have complained and demanded my own way.
I have whined about the places of discontent I have created.

I have not sought how to live by absorbing the examples YOU have given to me in it, gently nudging me toward insight and possibility.
YOUR WORD is relevant.
I have lived by my own light too long.
I turn from my own pursuit of significance and lie down.
I give YOU my allegiance afresh and anew to KNOW YOUR WORD.
Yea, Lord, to love it is to make it mine.
I want to live my life resting upon YOUR WORD.
Forgive my neglect.
Revive my weary soul.
Prod me daily to investigate and embrace YOUR Promises.
They are my pillows.
Jesus, I come.

Chapter Seven

A WALKING FAITH

Take a step.
Faith must progress.

I have always enjoyed prowling around antique shops to view what life looked like in past generations.

They were always collecting, saving, and deliberately preserving pieces of life that mattered to families, in the hope that somewhere down the line in the future, it would bring comfort, delight, and a sense of permanence to someone searching for it.

Treasured china tea cups, a ladies' writing desk, dolls, books, jewelry, a favorite chair, an heirloom quilt all seem to earmark what they valued.

Their possessions were a scrapbook of living that was to be cherished and cared for diligently and then passed on to another.

They gathered and made with their hands.

We collect stuff and then throw it away.

The family portraits are strikingly solemn, especially the wedding photos, which are usually proper, formal and sparse in expression as if the posing for it was painful. The female clothing undergarments in some instances squeezed the life out of you.

The faces were stoic, postured and encapsulated in time.

Vintage photographs have always awakened a longing in me.

My parents' baby pictures are so dear. Even though they are in sepia tones, I can imagine mother's silk leggings in a shade of delicate mossy green. She is seated and dressed in a matching crocheted hat and sweater. Her countenance is angelic, an expressive look framed by large deep set eyes. Dad's photo is the image of a contented, sleeping, robust baby with hands clasped together. He is lying in the seat of an over-sized, elaborately carved oak rocking chair bounded on both sides with large pillows trimmed in lace.

Looking at them as children brings me great comfort.

In years to come as my parents moved out of the family home, I would have more photos and memorabilia to ponder as the story of my father's family unraveled.

I remember the day Dad brought down a brown box from the attic to give to me.

He said, "This was Billy Hugh's. Do what you want to with it."

In a moment I came face to face with my namesake, who was killed in a tragic accident where two fourteen year old boys out in the woods in the country were playing with guns.

They did not know one of the guns was loaded.

In an instant Billy Hugh's life ebbed away that day in the arms of my grandmother, Isabella.

He was cherished by all.

So tragic was this loss and so deep was the pain that my father felt his name had to be carried on, so I was chosen.

Billy became Billie.

In the box was a snapshot of him sitting on a grassy bank with his collie Tony Tognetti (yep, that was the dog's name) resting under one arm. Billy Hugh was wearing overalls and a beige farmer's shirt. His face had brightness, a wide smile, fair skin, laughing eyes and unruly curly hair that tumbled over his forehead – very likable. No doubt he would have been quite handsome as his manhood flourished.

Next I saw a fertilizer card with his name on it. Perhaps it was a discount on a good deal. After all they farmed for a living. Ironically there was a toy cap gun and an old report card with conduct marks revealing that he was talkative. Yes, we were related. The last item was a New Testament which bore his name on the inside and it was obvious to me that it had been read, used, kept safe. I felt when I turned the pages that Billy Hugh had come to Christ and had learned how to walk with Him even though his time on earth was limited to only fourteen years.

His death brought spiritual life to my grandmother, known by me as Mama Bella.

She married at fifteen, had three children and then went back and got her certificate for high school graduation and enrolled at Blue Mountain College for Women in Mississippi.

Mama Bella became a teacher in a one-room schoolhouse in Burnsville, Mississippi, where she taught five different grades.

Her intense grief over the loss of Billy drove her to the Bible and she cried out to God for she had no where else to go.

She wrote poetry to lift her soul.

One day when I read her essay describing the reality of Christ's death, burial and resurrection, I knew she had a walking faith.

My husband listened as I read it out loud. He said, "You could have written that."

Faded photographs and written words speaking of lives walking in faith.

The formal portrait of these grandparents in their youth is now in my guest room.

My grandfather, Charlie Roane, could barely read.

His ruddy face, splashed with dashing good looks, intense eyes, and an expressive mouth, was interrupted by the same tousled unruly hair that his son Billy possessed.

My Grandmother Isabella's exquisitely fair, porcelain skin was her best feature. A high forehead framed by wisps of dark hair pulled back into a chignon and inquisitive, hazel eyes gave her an intelligent, determined look. Her nose was a bit long and her mouth a bit thin to be a real beauty.

I must confess I looked into the mirror of the past and saw me.

It was a "walk back" that affirmed a "walk forward."

There lived faith, tragedy, hard times, perseverance and overcoming.

Her antique cherry bed now resides in a guest room along with portraits of my four granddaughters, Cassidy, Tatum, Phoebe and Ella Joy, dressed in Victorian clothing. The portrait legacy of great grandparents, Granny Fox and John Henry, have also found resting places along side Mama Bella's favorite Victorian floral lamp. A wine colored jacquard chaise lounge, draped by a Lancaster County Amish quilt patterned in shades of rose and teal, accompanied by teddy bears and dolls, invites me to visit the past regularly.

Just walking into this room refreshes me.

It is positioned directly across from my study where I am writing today.

When I need a break, I stretch out in this spot and remember the faithfulness of God, the beginnings of faith, the journey of those who have gone before me and I am stirred to take my place in the lineup of a walking faith.

The knowledge of the past does impact the future.

I love antiques because they are reflective echoes,

But I must live in today.

The present must find its way to a walking faith.

The tall case antique French clock in the foyer downstairs strikes the hour. The melodious resonating dark tone finds its way up to my study, inviting me to stop and reflect on someone who is walking out her faith today in creative ways. A precious daughter in the Lord named Hope is a loving support to her dear husband Will while she homeschools her daughters Grace and Faith. This week she penned some thoughts about her life which lifted the weight I was carrying. After reading them, I felt as though I had had a personal visit from my heavenly Father and He had reminded me that my weight was from Him therefore He would carry it for me. I have mentored Hope. Today it was my turn to be mentored.

She wrote, "I believe God was glorified in my 'yesterday' so in my time with Him this morning I wanted to share a few thoughts with you. As I was trying to recover from sickness, I woke up with an overwhelming need to put the house back together and get things up and running again. God seemed to impress me to 'Do the next thing' as Elisabeth Elliott says so wisely in her writings. Therefore I sat down and prioritized one thing at a time, responding to the order in which God had placed them within my mind. As lunch approached, I phoned Will to see if I should prepare lunch for him or if he was going to join us. Immediately I heard the distress in his voice. Currently in Will's business as a builder he has four houses on the market. He proceeded to tell me the calamities of the day thus far; a man had cursed him, someone else had not shown up for work, material had not been delivered and he personally was tarring a foundation at the same time while trying to 'put all these fires out.' I spoke a few words to encourage him and got off the phone to pray. I went to his desk and began weeping and crying out to my Father in heaven speaking in the Name of Jesus…asking for intervention, asking for God to move in this situation, to bring encouragement to Will's heart. I finished and called someone to stand in the gap with me…. The Lord laid it upon my heart to call a friend who lives in the neighborhood where he is building. There was no answer. I left a message. In three minutes, my phone rang and her daughter told me that they had received the message. My dear friend and her daughter jumped into the car and off they went where Will was working. In my message I told her the situation and my need. I asked her to 'feed my husband a sandwich for lunch and to feed his soul.' She arrived with a grilled cheese and tomato sandwich along with a frosty root beer. With laughter, he told her that she either had an unbelievable intuition or she had received a phone call from me. His head was lifted a little higher because he had received the love of the Lord.

In the meantime the girls and I got on our knees and called out to the Lord for daddy. I asked them for their ideas of what we might do for him when he came home. Grace said, 'Tidy the house. He likes a clean house.' I answered, 'You are exactly right, we'll do it.' Faith wanted to take a bath, wash her hair and they both wanted to put on Sunday dresses with bows in their hair to greet him when he walked in. I agreed, 'Yes, we'll do it.' Then I went about preparing a meal, setting the table out on the porch with a tablecloth and candles while putting on his favorite Dean Martin CD…. We waited…. He called to tell us it would be another ten minutes before he could come as he was showing Lot number one to somebody. We again ran to our prayer rug and prayed for this opportunity, for God to bring people to see them. The girls then waited at the door for their daddy. He walked in and they embraced him. They told him how much they loved him. Faith said, 'Can we get married today, Daddy?' It was the most precious moment I've ever witnessed. He smelled like tar. We sent him to the shower. We put dinner on the table. He came out in a tie! As we enjoyed our meal, we worshipped and thanked God in prayer.... The girls danced with him after dinner. I told him I hoped he had received a 'deposit in the marriage account' from me.... That was my intention...to honor the Lord and watch over the affairs of my household. When dinner was finished we got a call that an agent would be showing Lot two, another property of ours in the afternoon. God was working for us. As I went to bed, I thanked God for the power of the Holy Spirit that spoke into my life, guiding me to obey yesterday when I could have so easily made the day about me and the needs I had being sick, being needy.... God in His mercy and grace helped me to live the NEW SELF he is creating...maturing.... I am not boasting; for many years I lived out of the old self (and still do). I suffered so many consequences and missed such blessings. No, I haven't arrived. Quite the contrary, but I have more desire to learn than ever before.... The Truth sets you free. What is the truth about marriage? My marriage is to GLORIFY GOD. I am to place Will's needs before my own. I am created to be his HELPMEET. I am to display respect even when I do not feel like it. My agenda is to receive what God is trying to accomplish in the life of my husband and children, to become more myself. I was to do what is best for the Glory of God so HE can be lifted up."

When I finished reading this "scenario of faith lived out" because of living under the authority of a loving, orchestrating God, a fresh supply was released to me and I advanced.
Condemnation is not from God.
Circumstances can swallow us.
Conviction compels us to ask and seek God's mind on a matter and then to do it.
Hope did.
So did I.

A life that lives by prayer encounters God.
A life that is penitent has discovered its own weaknesses.
A life that receives from God is creative.
A life that believes God is active in all things can rely on His timing

A life that depends on God can wait for the answer.
A life that trusts in His Truth brings Glory to Him.

This is walking faith.
The times of my grandparents are not my times but the same God is hovering.
So I got up and walked downstairs and sat in my maternal grandmother Offie's
wing-back chair, which I now have, and thanked God for her walk of faith.
I felt at home and at rest with the Creator who chose my lineage and urged me
from childhood to walk with Him.
There were steps to take.
There still are.
I can learn every day.
So can you.
We must receive from one another.
I still believe that "all that is needed to change the world is one man or woman
totally given into God's hands." (1)
The words of this hymn came forth:

Come ye that love the Lord,
And let your joys be known,
Join in a song of sweet accord,
Join in a son of sweet accord
And thus surround the throne and thus surround the throne.

Simple faith in the Savior brings rest.

Most gladly therefore will I rather glory in my infirmities that the power of Christ may
rest upon me. (2)

When His power is resting upon me, I can walk.

ARRESTING THOUGHTS

1.   Does your family legacy reveal faith or fear?

2.   What step today would bring you closer to a walking faith?

3.   Does the power of Christ rest upon you? If not, why not?

REST ASSURED

"Each day comes bearing its own gifts.
Untie the ribbons."
– Faith Baldwin

A PILLOW PRAYER

Beloved Father;
We long to live in peace with the assurance that YOU are there.
Sometimes we must look back before we can look forward.
Thank YOU for the evidence of godliness in generations past.
Some of their struggles are ours today.
We want homes that are built on a foundation of trust and faith.
Husbands and wives need to respect and love one another.
Give us a divine creativity as we ponder how to demonstrate YOUR LOVE.
We must lean into YOUR Word for guidance and then follow YOUR promptings, YOUR nudges to give.
Some have no spiritual legacy, but YOU can begin with them.
Encourage them to believe, to take a step and then to walk.
As we walk in faith today, we rest in YOU.
Keep us moving in obedience toward the high calling of life lived in Christ Jesus.
In His Name we bow down.

Chapter Eight

CHANGING YOUR STRIDE

Life has rhythms.
Faith moves.

I walk for exercise, strength, time alone and space with God.
Today I awakened with a compelling GO.
I was filled with an urgency to get dressed, get my shoes on and my favorite straw hat, cell phone and sun glasses, and get outside into the clean fresh air where birds sing, dogs bark and trees live.
I was depleted and God knew it.
It was a sultry summer day with droplets of perspiration already forming on my neck within the first ten minutes of my morning walk. The earth was parched and desperately yearning for rain. My soul was weighted down with many concerns and it was crying out for respite. As I turned a corner a brisk breeze began to kick up causing me to grab my hat! The sound of its movement surprised me; it was like the "rush of a wind a'comin." The pear trees along my route were swaying, creating a rippling wave as I passed. Then I seemed to be swept up into a musical refrain as a singular bird began to serenade me with such clear, pure, and lyrical warbling that I wanted to stop and sit down on a park bench just to listen.
But I didn't.
The benches always look so inviting and I think about it as I go by but I never stop.
After all this was a walk.
The birdsong trailed after me.
I could not find him but I could hear him.
He found me.
He tailed me.
He was sent to find me.
Within moments, my heavy heart poured out its anguish to my Lord as hot tears spilled over running down my cheeks. I laid my burdens down; an aging, frail mother with a broken body close to Heaven's gate, close friends battling

cancer, a family prodigal looking for instant gratification, grandchildren with dreams, so many directions in which to go – the known and the unknown.

My weeping became worship unto a Sovereign God who was tracking me with a bird whose mission was to sing to me.

Bird on assignment.

As I continued to walk I was glad that I was wearing sunglasses that not only shielded me from the glare of sun but also gave me a private look at the world around.

A stillness came.

The cadence of the air calmed and I slowed my gait and began to notice earthworms wiggling their way from one side of the sidewalk to the other.

A heavy rain during the night had deposited moisture enough for some to travel.

Some had expired trying.

Some were still in the process of contending.

Some were waiting for a signal.

I could identify with them.

Expiring, grappling, waiting.

Pondering their plight, I rounded a corner and a fresh wind gust whipped my shirttail up and nearly took my hat once again. In the distance toward the east I saw a flash of lightning and in a few seconds thunder clapped her hands. A band of sputtering, grey clouds were promising to shower the earth, as had been done last night.

I knew I had better head for home.

The first rain drops fell gently and then they flowed into a pelting downpour.

I had to change my stride.

It was now a combination of walk and run, walk and run, sloshing through puddles waiting for me.

Within seconds the bottom fell out of the sky and I was in a blinding downpour.

I managed to tuck my cell phone into the bosom of my shirt with the hope that it might survive the deluge.

Significance, right?

My sunglasses were prescription lenses so I need them to see but I couldn't see with them on and I couldn't see with them off.

My straw hat began to wilt and the multi-ribboned band which I had painted very artistically with several shades of pink, purple, red, yellow, and green was now a rivulet of color bleeding into my hair and running down my face.

The reason I became aware of this phenomenon is because I raised my hand to hold on to my hat and when I took it down it was dripping purple.

It startled me.

I must have looked pitiful because a compassionate Honda driver stopped to offer me a ride.

I shook my head as to communicate "no thanks,"

although...I came close to accepting.

With my mind focused on the last three blocks before rushing home, I breathed in deeply and began to thank God for getting me closer every minute.

I was soaked through and through.

My shoes squeaked with water.

And suddenly as I crossed the next intersection, the rain stopped as if a switch had been flipped.

With another block to go, I sat down on one of those benches and breathed in a fresh vitality.

And guess what?

I spied earthworms lining up haphazardly, but this time they were in a full court press making their way across the sidewalk. They come up for air when it rains because moisture is the vehicle in nature that helps them cross over the hard porous concrete surface to the other side.

Once there, they began tunneling once again.

"Their tunnels provide the soil with passageways through which air and water can circulate, and that's important because soil microorganisms and plant roots need air and water just like we do." (1)

They have five hearts, reproduce like rabbits and can reconfigure to elongate their bodies or to or scrunch up like a ball, whichever is needed.

Wish we could do that.

We need earthworms.

Earthworm faith works.

We need to come up for air, to take a break, to listen to the world of nature, to walk in the rain and allow it to wash away the toxins of fear and fatigue.

Then, in obedience, go back and tunnel through.

I arose from the bench, holding my arms as high as I could into the sky thanking God for this epiphany and walked slowly, deliberately the rest of the way to my front door.

I was at peace.

My husband, Roy, had just gotten up to meet the day oblivious to the summer cloudburst. When he saw me, he burst into a gale of laugher and said, "Hi, honey; I think you got caught in the rain, right?"

When I looked in the mirror and saw my rainbow hair, I laughed.

Bedraggled

Bewildered

Blessed, I was.

Lifted into the Presence of God,
Showered by His Love,
I can see clearly now, the rain must fall.

Sometimes we wander into a place that was designed to be a sanctuary where
the quiet reveals the noise in our souls and yet stirs us to move toward God.
In St. Leo, Florida, on the campus of St. Leo University, I was privileged to
spend an afternoon at The Holy Name Monastery. As I drove to and fro
during the week speaking at women's ministry events, my eye caught the words
"monastery" on the church marquee out front.
Public speaking requires purposeful withdrawal.
I was tired and it was time to do so.
My hostess had a hair appointment scheduled during this busy week and wanted
to know what I wanted to do on that day. Without a hesitation, I said, "Drop
me off at the monastery." She gave me an amused look, smiled and said, "Okay,
I should be gone a couple of hours or less but I will call you."
I was elated because I wanted to go soak in some silence.
Upon arriving, I ambled over to the gift shop and looked at the books. I spoke
to the Monk in charge and thoroughly enjoyed talking with him about the
area. It was my desire to let him know that I was going to visit the chapel, walk
the grounds and enjoy the peaceful pause. My goal was to make sure he knew
I was a fellow pilgrim, not an intruder. When I left the store, I had purchased
two books written by Thomas Merton and Basil Pennington for myself and I
left a couple of books I had written for the monks to read. He assured me they
would do so in devotions.
The day was incredible, clear, inviting and mine.
I began my contemplation by sitting down on a bench positioned near the
front door to the Abbey. Massive shade trees abundant with Spanish moss
encompassed the courtyard. The trickling of the fountain's rhythm was
mesmerizing. Small white chairs were nested together as if to invite strangers
to sit and muse. The church chimes rang out, heralding the coming hour
with certainty but they were also a call to stop, to cease, to be aware of time
passing.
Birds fluttered overhead, I rested and breathed in the air of tranquility.
I watched two young mothers engage in conversation while one picked up her
crying baby girl from a stroller, the other one was trying to corral her small
sons who were running round in circles, laughing, aggravating each other and
playing chase.
Scenes of mothering, oh, how I remember.
Then two young men, perhaps in late teens or early twenties, walked up together

and pulled up two of the white chairs and sat down. They opened their books and began an animated discussion. It was obvious they were students at St. Leo's and it was clear they were enjoying the exchange of ideas. In a few moments they prayed together.

A picture of college days and the thirst for knowledge held by God's thirst.

I drank it all in and then decided to go inside the chapel.

It was void of people but a lovely, lingering beauty entered as beams of filtered sunlight found their way through gothic doors.

I sat down in the front pew on the right and for a moment imagined the procession of men and women who had been influenced for God in this place. Before St. Leo's had become a church, it had another life. I discovered in reading a brochure that in 1889 it was a boarding school. By 1911 the property at St. Leo was acquired. This religious order of women did not have money to build so they decided to move the building one half mile uphill. Imagine this feat! Onlookers said that it could not be done but it was.

A minister was hired to do the construction. "The building was raised on log rollers; they encircled the house with a steel cable. With a winch and two oxen circling a dead man timber, buried fifty feet ahead of the house, it inched forward. They could only do one setting a day. It took six summer weeks…and the best part is the students and teachers all lived in it while the house was moved." (2) This called-out group of women was committed to community, the ministry of one another.

I reflected on the beginnings of faith here.

I thanked God for mine.

Then I opened my Bible to Psalm 89:1 and read it out loud in the hushed serenity.

Just God and me.

One audience.

I will sing of the Lord's great love forever; with my mouth I will make your faithfulness known through all generations.

There was a hallowed, unruffled solitude surrounding me as I spoke.

Then I sang words to an old hymn:

Holy Spirit breathe on me until my heart is clean,
Let sunshine fill its inmost part without a cloud between.
Breathe on me
Breathe on me.

Holy Spirit, Breathe on me.
Take thou my heart,
Cleanse every part.
Holy Spirit, breathe on me.

Because of the natural acoustics of the high ceiling, I soared in song and gently was led into God's presence.

When I finished singing, I was filled with a quiet wonder at God's plan to send Jesus to earth, to die for the sins of man – mine and yours and all who have lived or will live, for one perfect sacrifice made by HIS death, for the reality that I am His and HE is mine forever, for the Gospel to be translated and carried to all my brothers and sisters in Christ Jesus all over the world.

To Tennessee where I live,
To St. Leo, Florida,
To the jungles of Africa,
To the islands of the Caribbean,
To the Himalayas,
To the waterways of China...HE comes.

On and on the images of the nations came to mind as I visualized them receiving the wonderful gift of Jesus' Love and forgiveness through the Cross.

As I picked my Bible up the pages fell open to Psalm 85:6

Will you not revive us again, that your people may rejoice in you? (3)

My weariness entered worship.
I was centered.
Thomas Merton spoke of his desire "to pass through the center of his own soul and lose himself in the mystery...the transcendent reality of God." (4)

I had been gloriously recovered.
I walked outside and completed my afternoon sabbatical as I encircled the outer perimeter of the college. Classes were ending for the day and students were hurrying to get on their way home.
I recognized my friend's car driving up.
She looked lovely.
We each had been to the beauty shop.
My soul had been adorned.
I was made ready for the rigors of tomorrow.
In sunshine or rain, outside or inside, the momentum of faith must continue to move.

If we seek HIM we shall find Him though He *is not far from each one of us*. (5)
Sometimes we have to change our stride.
Musical words framed my mind:

All to Jesus I surrender.
All to Him I freely give.
I will ever love and trust Him.
In His presence daily live.
I surrender all.
I surrender all
All to Him, my blessed Savior,
I surrender all.

To surrender I must practice.
A musical rest is not to be slurred over.
It is placed in the measure to punctuate, to pause.
The melody of the Master's life brings rest.
In seeking we find.

ARRESTING THOUGHTS

1.   When was the last time you took a walk with God and came home refreshed?

2.   Do you allow the practical beauty of nature to remind you of His provision?

3.   Have you discovered the benefits of silence in your spiritual journey?

REST ASSURED

"I would rather live in a world where my life is surrounded by mystery
than live in a world so small my mind could comprehend it."
– Harry C. Fosdick

A PILLOW PRAYER

Holy God;
I need to take more walks with YOU, to breathe in YOUR Life when mine is worn out.
Show me how to be practical in my faith, to absorb the beauty around me.
Give me an awareness of the mystery of YOUR LOVE.
Let me move into the marvel of it.
Call me aside.
Give me a hunger for the silence that blots out the noise of the world.
Speak to me from YOUR WORD, through YOUR MUSIC.
Clear my vision from self effort and let me rest upon YOUR shoulder all of my cares.
Beloved comforter and Friend,
I come again in Jesus' Name.

Chapter Nine

PILLOW OF REVERENCE

God is holy.
Rest in HIM.

What do I revere?
To whom do I give reverence?
Where is my allegiance directed?

We were made to know God.

*Let not a wise man glory in his wisdom, let not the mighty man glory in his might,
let not the rich man glory in his riches; but let him who glories glory in this that he
understands and knows me. (1)*

God is holy, Other, set apart, worthy, venerated.
No other is in this category.
Yet HE knows you and me.

See, I have engraved you on the palms of my hands. (2)

Imagine what this might signify.
This is not a reference to your name although that would be pleasing.
This indicates that when HE looks at His Hands HE sees you and me but it
means more.
HE loves us.

I have loved you with an everlasting love. (3)

So our God knows, sees, and loves us.
And HE is to have our reverence.
Knowing Him is our highest joy for earnest zeal leads us to worship.
We were created to worship our God.

To know we have relationship in HIM points to the awesome reality of having fellowship with HIM.
HE is holy and we are to be holy.

You are to be holy to me because, I the Lord am holy and I have set you apart from the nations. (4)

What a family inheritance we have.
This astounding connection is what brings us to faith, liberty, purity and rest.
HE who is holy knows no sin,
But we do sin.
HE cannot dwell where sin resides.
Therefore we must discipline our hearts to yearn for fellowship with this God to whom we owe reverence.
In our modern culture we observe the daily grind and regimen achievement demands.
Athletes train.
Singers sing.
Builders build.
Writers write.
We follow hard after our passions, sometimes getting burned out and diverted in the process.
Why?
Because the prize goes to the rich and famous, the beautiful and academic, the powerful and affluent.
The prize is recognition, ours.
How seductive is notoriety.
Subtly our eye wanders away from lofty goals and we are ensnared by the world's trophies forgetting the true prize, the high calling in Christ Jesus.
Our hearts compromise.
We become inward and self absorbed.
We are diligent in pursuing renovation of the outward person.
Plastic surgeons rid us of wrinkles.
Diets rid us of weight.
Exercise rids us of a sedentary life style,
But we cannot "Botox" our heart.
It must be rejuvenated from the inside out with the Word of God, washed clean by confession of sin, covered by the Blood of the Lamb, filled with God's Spirit, made acceptable for worship.
Historically the children of Israel knew all about this mandate.

Remembering the Sabbath day and keeping it holy was and still is a commandment.

It is a clarion call to establish worship as a holy habit.

They had to prepare for the Sabbath for there were rules to govern what could and could not be done.

There was to be no work on the seventh day.

God was revealing a type of pattern to them, one HE originated when HE created the world and rested on the seventh day.

God was not tired.

God chose to rest, commemorating the Sabbath as a holy day set apart to remember HIM.

We need to rest.

They understood that the work week would be six days,

Period.

They were to cease working on the seventh.

There has to be balance between work and rest.

Rules get broken and so Sabbath keeping became Catch Up day.

Wayne Muller in his book *Sabbath* says this:

"Our culture invariably supposes that action and accomplishment are better than rest, that doing something – anything – is better than doing nothing. If we refuse to rest until we are finished we will never rest until we die. Sabbath dissolves the artificial urgency of our days."

God set up the Sabbath to set us a part as His people.

You must observe my Sabbaths. This is a sign between me and you for the generations to come so that you may know that I am the Lord, who makes you holy (5)

Then Jesus came,

His life signaled a divine invitation to a Sabbath rest that all who believed could enter.

There remains a Sabbath rest for the people of God (6)

Jesus brought access to God.

Identity in Him birthed a longing to worship, to reverence a holy God.

Every time we purpose to give to HIM the honor and love due, we rest.

Our exhaustion becomes expectancy.

Our omissions become opportunities.

Our oppression becomes an offering,

And we are renewed, redefined again and again.

What we reverence we serve.

We can choose to remember or forget.

"The Sabbath trains us to notice the hand of God because our hands are still long enough for us to be inwardly changed.... We need to test in reality that our lives do not originate with us...the Sabbath calls us to experience that love and favor resting with God. It frees us from life destroying forces in the world...giving us an engaging rhythm, a musical beat that helps us step away from advertisements and media and competition and stress." (7)

But I, when I am lifted up from the earth, I will draw all men to myself. (8)

So when we observe the Sabbath, we begin Sabbathing.

God gives us Sabbath moments wherever we are.

Our minds can be brought into captivity with HIM in the car, at a dentist appointment, buying groceries, waiting for a friend.

"God's invitation to sabbath rest is an invitation to peace in the midst of feverish activity.... Sabbath time is a time when we imitate God by stopping and resting." (9)

Revering the King of Kings is a holy obedience required of a holy people but it is more.

It then becomes our pleasure to delight in HIM.

In lifting HIM up, we are lifted.

Sabbathing happens when we become true worshippers.

Reverence refreshes.

It was a day of pristine white sandy beaches and lapping Caribbean blue waters.

We were welcomed to the island of Tortola with the strings of guitars, bongo drums, and costumed dancers swirling around in cotton skirts patterned in exotic flowers of orange, red and yellow.

They were beckoning us to shop, swim, sit, enjoy.

It was hot.

Roy and I decided to walk toward the main street shopping area thinking we might dart in and out of air conditioning and breathe in some cool air.

No such luck.

Within a few minutes we were searching for any respite pit stop in which to hydrate for the humid walk back to the pier.

It was almost 100 degrees.

Obviously people were dressed in shorts allowing their bodies a level of comfort. I was wearing a hat which gave me some protection.

The sun was blazing.

Humidity was rising.

We were wilting.

This is the tropical heat one reads about or observes in a jungle movie but does not expect to experience it.

But we were experiencing it!

As we looked around at the faces of the people in the arcade, we were filled with a sense of loss.

Tourism is the livelihood of these islands.

Every day the people must shore up their despondency, get up and face strangers hoping their crafted wares will sell.

Income is needed.

The colorful garbs they wore did not hide the effects of economic decline and set-backs that storms had caused. There were construction projects everywhere half finished.

Hope deferred makes the heart sick. (10)

Yes, sick and tired and faint.

Poverty has a face one does not soon forget.

The last two blocks brought us to the flea market, a large group of individual vendors crammed together with tables side by side bearing all kinds of crafted memorabilia. There were beads, turtle sculptures, art work, prints, Tee shirts, hats, shells, spices, jams, soaps, rocks, plants, Johnny cakes and sodas. Overhead there was a makeshift tent attempting to shelter the direct rays of the sun for the workers. A few of them had resorted to umbrellas lined up as a temporary shield.

It was now a miserable sweltering heat, and beads of perspiration had formed under my hat and were running down my neck and forehead. Roy walked in one direction to get a coke and I walked in another to look at some fabric.

All around people were pushing their items trying to muster up enthusiasm they did not have for what was being hawked. In fact one man actually said, "Come and let me show you want you don't need" and then mischievously he managed a smile. Ironically his candor was so truthful that we followed him to his booth. I saw a turquoise shawl "clothes-pinned" to an umbrella down the way a bit so I veered toward it. I could hear sounds of recorded music playing in the background from a radio. I remember thinking that it must be battery operated because there was no electricity here.

No power.

Then I stopped because I recognized the music as a Christian song familiar to me.

It was the chorus, *In His Presence.*

What a comfort God's music brings with His Presence into this oppressive heat, reminding all of HIM.

I began to hum as I scouted for the source of the music and soon spied a boom box stashed in a corner on a table.

Beside it was a woman whose head was bowed down in prayer.

I watched her as she laid down her burdens.

Then quietly I joined her.

In a moment she was in worship, singing her praises to her Lord in the market place, singing with the radio.

So I joined her, a perfect stranger, yet one with Him.

When she heard me joining her, she walked toward me and greeted me with a contagious smile that spread across her caramel skinned face. Her head was tied up in a crisp white turbaned knot that accentuated her island bearing with dignity.

The weariness of her life had momentarily faded.

We had connected in faith.

We were sisters in the same family.

We blessed each other.

I purchased a wooden beaded necklace and left still singing of His comfort and peace. In the distance I could still hear His music continuing to permeate this depressed little shanty business mart where hope evaporates daily with the temperature,

Except in the people whom He has called to Himself,

They find a resting place wherever they are.

"The way to mend the bad world is to create the right world."
Ralph Waldo Emerson

What a Sabbath moment.

The heat was lifted and so were hearts that reverenced Him.

Holy is the Lord.

HE is worthy.

We are His people and HE is our God.

HE warns us.

Today if you hear His voice: Do not harden your hearts, as in the rebellion, as in the day of trial in the wilderness when your fathers tested Me, though they saw My work. For forty years I was grieved with that generation, and said, "It is a people who go astray in their hearts, and they do not know My ways." So I swore in My wrath. "They shall not enter my rest." (11)

A hardened heart blocks.
Rest is a reward.
Not every one can enter.

Almighty God is seeking people to worship Him. (12)

Anywhere we go, HE is there.

Sing His praise from the ends of the earth...You islands...Give glory to the Lord and declare His praise in the coastlands. (13)

And we did sing.

Holy, Holy, Holy!
Lord God Almighty!
Early in the morning our songs shall rise to Thee
Holy, Holy, Holy all the saints adore Thee...
Perfect in power, in love and purity.

Reverence is a pillow.
Rest in Him

ARRESTING THOUGHTS

1.   What kind of altar am I building?

2.   Is my exhaustion a product of "no reverence" for God?

3.   How does worship affect rest?

REST ASSURED

"Things that are holy are revealed only to men who are holy."
– Hippocrates

A PILLOW PRAYER

Faithful Father;
Too long has my heart been disengaged.
No wonder I am barren and depleted.
My altar is a revelation of false gods.
It is a stench unto YOU, Holy God.
I come and fall down in true confession.
Break open my hardened heart and cleanse me from self pursuit.
There is no holiness in me apart from YOU.
I come to YOU for the resurrection of worship
I owe homage to YOU ALONE.
I have failed.
I need to come home.
Jesus, YOU are near to the broken.
I come asking forgiveness.
I bow down in contrition.
I rise in reverence to The God of all gods, mine to honor forever.
Accept my worship I pray in the Holy Name of Jesus.

Chapter Ten

PILLOW OF EMBRACE

God is grace.
Rest in HIM.

I will always remember the first embrace from my Navy pilot husband, Roy, as he returned from a US Navy deployment during which we were separated for many months.
This was a scene repeated over and over in our thirty years of Navy life.
I never tired of rehearsing for it, imagining the isolation and loneliness of my life apart from Roy being washed away. Yes, washed away much like the constancy of the ocean's waves, ever familiar, faithful, and dependable.
The embrace was my first touch, reconfirmation of the bond of love.
I anticipated it.
I drew upon memory.
I longed for it.
Always, it brought more to me than I expected.
A 360 degree hug encircled by loving arms,
Encompassed, held, secure at last.
A great sigh of thanksgiving accompanied tears of joy.
"Lord, thank YOU for carrying me through once again by YOUR Grace."
Did I really understand the word "grace"?
I am sure I didn't but I believed I had experienced it and I knew it was tied to Jesus.
Sometimes you know more than you know and you don't know how.
You just know it.
Our intimacy with God is a love affair in grace.
The Bible gives us clues.

God opposes the proud but gives grace to the humble. (1)

It is good for your hearts to be strengthened by grace (2)

See to it that no one misses the grace of God and that no bitter root grows up to cause trouble and defile many. (3)

Be strong in the grace that is in Christ Jesus (4)

Every time I read words about grace I am conscious about what I must do to receive it.

My heart must be made ready, humbled, cleansed and then it will be strengthened by grace.

Grace is about supply and the supply comes to us through Christ Jesus.

I need simplicity.

Years ago I tried to think about how a homemaker might understand grace and appropriate it.

It would have to be practical application not a theological one.

This is what followed.

It is God's
> **R**esponse
> **A**nd
> **C**are
> **E**very day wrapped up in His character.

Grace is the divine equipping we need in order to live.

Equipping and supply I can comprehend.

My relationship as a child of God through Christ is where my supply begins.

I must know Jesus to have it.

I am His and HE is mine.

This I know.

His Word inspires and instructs me.

I trust in your word (5)

I begin with prayer.

Prayer is loving God back each day.

It is also the place of provision where I can go and ask for enough grace for the day, the trial, the work ahead.

As I love God back in prayer, my supply is given.

"Prayer galvanizes faith, moving it forward." (6)

I am then empowered for the task because I ask for my supply.

There will always be enough.

Grace and truth came through Jesus Christ. (7)

Grace is the equipping.
Truth is the standard.
Jesus is the source.
This is our assurance.
God carries His own through life with an unending supply of His grace.
His treasure chest marked "grace" is available to you and me.
But there is a preparation to be done.

I know my God that you test the heart and are pleased with integrity. (8)

Living in a grace supplied heart brings strength.
Therefore grace is the embrace of God, the pillow of HIS loving storehouse
It is keenly assimilated in triumph and tragedy.

Several years ago Roy and I were privileged to attend the debut of the *Titanic* art exhibit in Memphis.
We seem to be drawn to the strength and character of those who endure life's tests.
I wanted to digest some factual truth about this historical event, not just view another glamorization of a movie scenario.
This was the first time any of the artifacts taken from the ship had ever been shown to the public. As I walked into the exhibit, I breathed a prayer, "Lord, show me that YOU were there that day?"
It was an eerie experience to be carried along through creative tableaus reconstructing the day of the horror. A complete replica of the ship was on display.
There were cases of jewelry, clothing and newspaper articles in glass cabinets.
Music wove an enchanting melancholia, inviting us to absorb the impact of this historical event.
There will always be interesting stories surrounding this event with mystique, some fact and some fiction.
The Captain, E. J. Smith said, "Men, you have done your full duty and I release you. That's the way of it sometimes, every man for himself."
Words of strength.
Fact.
Artist Frances Milet wrote a letter, which arrived in Cherbourg the day before the sinking, using these words to describe American women, "There is a number of ostentatious American women, many of them carrying tiny dogs and leading their husbands around like pet lambs."
Words of perception.
Fact.

The song *Nearer My God to Thee* was sung as the ship went down and the *Lord's Prayer* was recited during the night.

Words of faith.

Fact.

There was an older couple named Mr. and Mrs. Strauss. She would not get into a life boat and leave her husband. She said," Mr. Strauss and I have lived many years together. Where you go, I go. As we have lived so shall we die."

Words of courage.

Fact.

In a newspaper article, a quote was given from the Captain of the *Carpathia*, the ship that rescued Titanic survivors. "Some other hand guided mine to the scene."

Words of grace.

Fact.

A hand of human embrace guided by a Hand of Divine Embrace reached out and saved 705 people.

They and their family lineage will carry a costly triumph with them all the days of their lives.

We carry a common thread with them.

We all must remember to embrace grace.

It was a gloriously crisp sunny December day. Our son, US Navy Chaplain Carey Cash, was flying into Fayetteville, NC for training and professional accreditation. We had the wonderful opportunity to fly there to spend a couple of days with him. He was stationed in Naples, Italy with his family and had been in Washington, DC on an assignment the week before for a certification.

We were excited and waiting for his plane to land, anxious for the first embrace of a beloved son we do not see very often.

When he appeared striding down the walkway, he started smiling and in a few moments we were into a three way body hug.

He looked terrific and was full of details, stories, and family news.

While in Washington DC, he had gone to Bethesda Naval Hospital to visit our wounded soldiers.

He went to give.

He received.

How courageous are those who embrace sacrifice.

The next couple of days with us were conference days for him so we met him for the meals.

It was blessed time for us.

Remembering family stories of his growing up were laced with gales of laughter and lots of hugs for we were held in the embrace of grace.

The last day we were with him, Roy and I were relaxing, drinking coffee and waiting for Carey to come to lunch.

Looking outside on the patio windows, I was drawn into reverie as I began to think of his homecoming with Charity and the children. He had been gone for two weeks. Christmas was coming.

There would be a long international flight ahead and I was feeling the motherly tug of reminiscence which occupies military life.

Thoughts bombarded me.

Tomorrow, Carey will go back to his God-ordained path of study and preparation to be God's man in this world. What joy for him to look forward to going home to his family.

Remembering renews.

My mind wandered back to a place of sanctuary created with my Lord that reminded me of the years where there was such space and aloneness that if I had not entered into it I would not have learned the wonder of release.

What did I learn?

Release of expectation.

Release of anxiety.

Release of all.

Every time I would let go and let God, I could rest in His Embrace.

Even today I still whirl ideas into motion.

I plan.

I sort.

I work.

But I can make nothing happen.

When I feel my surroundings are spinning emotionally I ask myself this question;

Is there any absolute I can know from day to day, any surety in which I have refuge?

Yes.

For today I remembered with sweeping awareness the impression of my Savior's Hand upon my shoulder as the great absences of Roy became concert halls where music played and I was the only audience.

These were places of quiet so deafening, the only sound was the sigh of my heart's longing,

A longing that coveted an intimacy in Christ Jesus that became the satisfaction of my soul.

Here I found the rest I craved, the peace I yearned for, the tranquility needed to settle and establish me.

My people will live in peaceful dwelling places, in secure homes, in undisturbed places of rest. (9)

I found a place of rest.

Under His wings you will find rest. (10)

Have you created a place within, a place to meet God?
"Finding a spacious place involves going away with Him in our hearts, leaving the distractions of this world, and focusing on the Lord – right where we are in life." (11)
I have.
Today as I mulled over these things in my heart, my friend Peggy came to mind for she was scheduled for chemo this week.
I am part of the calm that God has prepared to help her embrace the tumult, the tide of torment – again.
"Holy God, YOU are ELOHIM.
YOU create, move and change but there is a place of constant rest."
I know about it.
I had to find my way.
I am there.
It is the secret place where grace abides.
Yes, grace is an embrace.
Yet we seem to resist.
My awesome octogenarian friend Wayve Berg Bradley shares her thoughts.
"The rest of the believer is a great subject to pursue. Jesus calls us to rest no matter the circumstances. I remember years ago when my heart changed from resisting to rest... The holy bells of heaven rang in my heart and mind. In the desert of life's calamities, look for God's oasis of comfort. Faith is grace percolating."
She is, indeed, doing just that and so must we.
In Philip Yancey's book *What's So Amazing About Grace?* We hear this startling statement,
"There is nothing you can do to make God love you more.
There is nothing you can do to make God love you less."
Grace is not about you and me.
Grace is about God.
Perhaps that is why it is so hard to define.
God's perspective is not ours for ours is limited, finite.
His supply to us is filled to overflowing with Divine influence, favor and loving kindness, the complete accouterment of God.
But grow in grace and knowledge of our Lord and Savior Jesus Christ. (12)

We are challenged to grow in grace.

How?

By faith.

"Why are you cast down, O my soul? Why are you disquieted within me? Hope in God, for he is a God of matchless grace…HE sustains by grace…. You cannot earn it. It is free. Believe it. Rest in it. Delight in it and it is yours." (13)

Remembering resuscitates the mind.

It was balmy, blue-sky Caribbean day aboard our ship at sea, a day of rest and relaxation. About 2 pm, Roy and I wandered into a Pizza Parlor. There was pizza of every kind – cheese, sausage, pepperoni, vegetable, you name it. The crust was thin and crispy and we were hungry. We found a place to sit down and a young woman came over to take our order. I was not looking up when she came to the table but Roy was and he said, "What a lovely name you have!"

Then I did look up.

Our server who looked to be about twenty years old had a pleasant full smile, thick dark hair pulled back into a pony tail, animated brown eyes and flawless almond skin.

Small in stature, she was adorable.

Her ID badge indicated that her name was indeed "Lovely". It listed her country as The Philippines. When I saw her name I smiled and instantaneously, without another thought, said, "I bet when you were born, your mother held you up to God and thanked him for her lovely child and then she named you Lovely." With a twinkle in her eyes, she exclaimed, "You must be a believer!" It took me by surprise but with delight I matched the vigor of her response and said, "Yes indeed, we both are!"

Then with momentum she had to make sure if we were on the same playing field with our terms and she said, "You are a believer in Jesus Christ, right?"

I said, "RIGHT!"

One minute we were strangers.

The next we were members of the same family by the grace of God.

She told me that she had been on the ship two months and these were her words, "I must hang on to Jesus every day."

I asked her if she was married or single and discovered that she had been in love but the young man was not a believer so she knew they were not to wed.

We talked about the qualifications of a godly marriage.

So she knew the truth of the verse: *Do not be yoked together with unbelievers….* (14)

It was an encounter that God arranged.

Lovely needed a mother to confirm some things which she felt to be true.

By grace God arranged an embrace.
When we said goodbye, I hugged my sister in Christ and promised to send a book to her the next day to build her faith, to encourage her to follow Jesus. We ate scrumptious pizza but we were strengthened by embracing one another.
"Am I living a life valuing grace?" (15)

Remembering reclaims and once again a hymn's music came to me:

Twas grace that taught my heart to fear and grace my fear relieved.
How precious did that grace appear the hour I first believed.

My friend Peggy reveals insight when she says, "I realized more emphatically the grace I had yesterday is not enough for today; therefore it must be appropriated every day like our daily bread."
The grace of God is a treasured cache, a pillow to embrace.
We rest in HIM.

ARRESTING THOUGHTS

1.   Have you ever considered grace to be a supply, a divine equipping available to you?

2.   When we encounter people, is it possible that we become a part of the supply for someone else?

3.   Do you view your life as being "led by grace"? If not why not?

REST ASSURED

"Whenever anything begins to disintegrate your life in Jesus Christ, turn to Him at once and ask Him to establish rest."

Oswald Chambers

A PILLOW PRAYER

My Beloved Father;
I know YOU are always waiting for me to embrace the day by embracing YOU.
I remember moments of sweet communion when I took time to be with YOU.
I remember times that I ran from any attempt to re connect with YOU.
Self-effort is exhausting.
Forgive me.
I need grace.
For when I am spent from struggling for answers, YOU woo me to the pillow of grace.
Life can seem impossible.
God of the possible.
YOU lovingly dispense grace but I must ask.
Thank YOU.
Every time I act upon belief, my fatigue dissipates and I am carried, held, hugged.
YOU fill up my empty places with holy contentment and I am centered once again.
I rest in Jesus' Name.

Chapter Eleven

PILLOW OF SUFFICIENCY

God is able.
Rest in HIM.

In the movie, *The Chronicles of Narnia*, we are thrust into the exploits of a family of siblings; Lucy, Edmund, Susan and Peter, who are sent to live on the rural country estate of an aging professor. It is World War II in England. They are homesick for their parents but have been sent away to a safer place far from the blackouts and dangerous bombings. The children find themselves isolated and clinging to one another to survive.

One day while playing a game of hide-and-seek, Lucy scrambles to find a good hiding place, searching through the many rambling rooms.

She opens a door and finds herself staring at an ominous, singular wardrobe looming in the center of an otherwise empty room.

Pondering its enormity she comes and stands in amazement.

Should she go inside or keep running?

Lucy decides to take the risk.

She opens the door and enters a magical fortress filled to overflowing with fur coats that swished as she moved amongst them.

Her child's play leads her to forget the reason she came.

Time closes the door unnoticed, but her inquiring imagination leads her into the Land of Narnia, filled with adventures of good and evil.

Eventually her brothers and sister joined her and so did we.

The wardrobe became a symbol, a stronghold, a fortress, a citadel, a place of comfort and rest.

To find rest we must enter in.

Teach us to number our days that we may gain a heart of wisdom. (1)

Our days are numbered.
Our trials are ordered.
Our safety is in God's Hands.

If this is true, HE is sufficient, completely able.
Therefore HE is Sovereign.
It is true.
Webster defines sovereign as "supremacy of authority or rule."
We need His authority, His rule in order to rest.

The Lord has established his throne in heaven, and his kingdom rules over all. (2)

When we live under this principle we discover that HE is a Stronghold in the day of trouble.

While visiting Ft. Walton Beach, Florida last year around the Fourth of July, I decided to take an early morning walk. We were staying in quarters at Hurlburt Air Force Base, the home of the US Air Force Special Operations Forces. A huge permanent display of airplanes was decorated with flags and draped with red, white and blue bunting. One could not pass by without being drawn to investigate the heroism of these who lost their lives as they defended this nation in war.

I was compelled to stop.

The history of the First Commando unit was established in 1942-43 at the defeat of the Japanese at Burma.

The monument to their fallen heroes read, "Be assured we will go with you boys anytime, anywhere." Excerpts from their creed followed, "I am a Commando... my allegiance is to God...when I can't walk another step, I'll walk another mile with freedom as my goal." Then my eyes fell to words from scripture found in Isaiah 6:8.

Then I heard the voice of the Lord saying, 'Whom shall I send? And who will go for us?' And I said, 'Here am I. Send me!'

The aircraft had names with designations worth remembering, like: HH-3H Jolly Green Giant, The AC-119 Flying Box Car, A-6 Counter Invader, C-123 Provider, A-1E Skyraider, C-47 Skytrain/Gooney Bird, T-28 Trojan, and C-130 Hercules. The C-47 Gooney Bird had a unique inscription which read, "Shot down almost beyond recognition but never obliterated." Berlin airlift, Korea, Southeast Asia.

And then I came to a Medal of Honor winner, First Lieutenant James Philip Fleming. He flew the helicopter VH-1F for the 20th Special Operations squadron. In May of 1970, Fleming flew to aid a six-man Green Beret Special Forces long-range reconnaissance patrol in Duc Co, Viet Nam. They were in danger of being overrun by a large hostile force. He descended to rescue and had to balance his helo on the bank of the river with its tail boom hanging over the open water with complete disregard for his safety. He remained in an exposed position until the entire patrol could board.

They lived.

My tears begin to fall as I stood in sweltering heat. I was prompted to bow my head and thank God for these brave men who were a Stronghold of protection for one another, for our nation.

What a picture of sufficiency.

What a time of unsettling animosity.

What a presidio of surety.

Once again scriptures were engraved on stone to mark outwardly a bedrock belief in the destiny and devotion to an All Sufficient God.

You have seen how I have carried you on eagles' wings and brought you to myself. (3)

The last enemy to be destroyed is death. (4)

We who are still alive and are left will be caught up together with them in the clouds to meet the Lord in the air. (5)

I walked away and rested in this revelation.

In the immediate distance I could see an unusual triangular-shaped glass window in the building just in front of me. Upon entering the door a blast of air conditioning welcomed me and gratefully I sat down on a bench in front of the commemorative window. It had been placed there as a tribute to these men of valor. The artistic rendering in leaded glass before me was a globe of the world surrounded with penetrating rays of light shaded in the primary colors of blue, red and yellow intricately pieced together bursting forth like comets. A mammoth eagle was poised at the corner ready to encircle and rescue.

Underneath the eagle's feet was a crest of America.

As sunlight streamed through the window, ribbons of light slashed across the world as the constant eye of the eagle presented a critical vigilance.

Inscribed below were these words, "any place, and any time."

God is our refuge and strength
A very present help in trouble.
Therefore we will not fear.
The Lord of hosts is with us;
The God of Jacob is our stronghold. (6)

Stronghold,
Sovereign,
Sufficient,
This is our God.
We can learn how to live under authority by living in the Word of God.

Have you entered the storehouses…which I reserve for times of trouble? (7)

God's Word is a storehouse.

The Most High is sovereign over the kingdoms of men. (8)

So practically speaking, God is in control.
I am not,
Neither are you.
The Bible was given to us to reveal the life Christ poured out and delivered through the lives of real people who struggled to follow Him while in the midst of fear and fatigue.
Both assault and blessing come to the Stronghold of God,
Assault against it,
Blessing in it.

Consider the lives of two sisters, Rachel and Leah.
One is beautiful and one is not.

Leah had weak eyes but Rachel was lovely in form, and beautiful. (9)

Rachel was younger than Leah.
Jacob loved Rachel and worked seven years to have her as his wife.
Both ended up married to the same man.
Deliberate deception by a father-in-law named Laban gave Leah to Jacob on the wedding night, after seven years of work.
The discussion that followed revealed why.

It is not our custom to give the younger daughter in marriage before the older one. (10)

Jacob was then told to finish the bridal week with Leah and then Rachel would be his the following week but he would still have to work another seven years.
Rachel was always his choice, not Leah.

This story seems hard to comprehend, archaic, filled with delusion and self pandering.

But listen to the words of scripture:

When the Lord saw that Leah was not loved, he opened her womb but Rachel was barren. (11)

The Lord *saw* Leah was unloved.

HE sees us, hears our cries, watches over us until we are ready to enter His Stronghold.

His ways are not ours.

Leah began to bear sons and with each one she hoped to gain her husband's love.

She did not.

When the fourth son was born, she named him Judah.

It was from this tribe that Jesus would come.

Two more sons and a daughter came later.

Rachel became jealous and gave her maidservant, Bilhah, to Jacob and a son was born.

Then Leah gave her servant, Zilpah, to Jacob and a son was born.

The competition, the striving, the manipulation of women to get what they want is not unknown marital strife.

Finally, Rachel conceived and bore Joseph who would be in the lineage of Christ.

Both sisters bore sons who would be in the line of the Holy Messiah.

In the midst of this chaotic frazzled self-effort to get love, we hone in on some practical truth.

We can't make anyone love us.

We find fulfillment in God alone.

HE allows our insecurities and disappointments to crush us so that we will be weaned from wanting to will our way and wooed to a love that never dilutes life.

On our own we scheme and scream, faint and fall.

The assault will come.

We are incomplete by ourselves.

We can try to do it our way,

Or we can walk in the sufficiency of Christ Jesus, resting in the sovereign authority of God.

And you have been given fullness in Christ, who is the head over every power and authority. (12)

When Leah "began to please God...her soul began to change and enter God's stronghold...a true inner beauty started growing in Leah; she became a woman at rest." (13)
And so can we.
How do I know?
The Bible tells me so.
It was deliberately decreed that the law was to be read.
When a king took the throne he was admonished to do so.

It is to be with him. And he is to read it all the days of his life so that he may learn to revere the Lord his God. (14)

We do not always choose God's law.

"His own opinion was his law."
John Milton

We are privileged now to have access to the whole Bible.
We can choose to read the Bible.
We don't have to, we "get to."
It presents life lived from the Stronghold of God.
Blessing comes.

Time passed.
The years that followed encompassed many seasons of life including the deaths of Rachel and then Leah. Jacob spoke on his deathbed, "*I am about to be gathered to my people; bury me with my fathers in the cave...which Abraham bought as a burial place...there with Abraham and his wife Sarah, there Isaac and his wife, Rebekah were buried, and there I buried Leah.*" (15)
Jacob's favor came for Leah at last, for she was buried in the ancestral grounds of Abraham.
We read about it in the Word of God.
Stories remind us that in every generation there is a search for approval and a struggle to surrender our will.
Living in the Word of God we live in His Stronghold.
Even from my childhood, these words ring true today:

Jesus loves me this I know, for the Bible tells me so,
Little ones to Him belong, they are weak but He is strong...

And from God's Word we read:

I will lay me down in peace, and take my rest: for it is thou,
Lord that makes me dwell in safety. (16)

In honoring God, we please HIM.
In pleasing HIM, we find rest.
It is the pillow of sufficiency.
Rest in HIM.

ARRESTING THOUGHTS

1.   Is the Word of God a pragmatic guide for you?

2.   Is there rest in His Authority?

3.   What do you need to do in order to live in His Stronghold?

REST ASSURED

"What is more at Rest than the single eye?
And what is more free than he that desireth nothing upon earth?"
– Thomas A. Kempis

A PILLOW PRAYER

Sufficient Savior;
I believe.
Sovereign Lord, I now receive.
Fears unearthed throughout the years,
Fall before YOUR Throne with tears.
Living in YOUR WORD will be
A call to faith, a grace in me.
Secure, surrounded I shall see.
The Stronghold of Security.
Christ Alone is my portion, now and forevermore.

Chapter Twelve

PILLOW OF TRANSFORMATION

God is beauty.
Rest in HIM.

It was a week filled with angst, raw emotion, confusion, physical weakness and a pervading helplessness which translated into bone weariness.
I was more than just tired.
I was broken.
A feeling of fretful futility began to sweep over my psyche.
My emotions seemed to be registering impressions, words of caution, "quit, it's too much, you are going down."
And I was.
Exhaustion is exhausting.
We were getting my 82 year old mother ready for a surgical procedure which would strengthen a fracture and stabilize her spine.
There was a lot surrounding all of us,
Medications, tests, mental prep, doctor's appointments, spiritual release.
Looking back,
Looking forward,
Finally settling into the present moment.
She was frail.
I was frightened.
It would be a long day.
Words of hope, love and promise were spoken.
Then the wait began.
We entered the hospital at 11:00 am and left at 6:00 pm.
The day progressed slowly.
Finally, mother went home and so did I.
Once I walked inside, I collapsed into the over-stuffed moss-green sofa in the keeping room and thought about staying there forever.
It is a comfortable piece of furniture with deep sides, a high curved back, flanked with cushioned pillows used to prop up whatever body part needs it.

The sofa enfolds you.

When you add a favorite quilt to wrap up in, you have entered the land of Nod with random thoughts of perhaps never leaving this place of comfort.

Spent and poured out, I also needed spiritual oxygen.

Later that night I checked phone messages and there was one from a precious new friend named Ginger, who had been my secret "Gal Pal" for months.

She did not know it but God did.

HE had put us together.

Everyone who agreed to participate in this project was to become an encourager to her "Pal" through notes, gifts and most of all prayer every day.

It was pure joy for me.

I loved her the moment God placed her into my life.

This was designed to foster friendship among the women in our couples' class at church.

At the end of the year we would reveal to one another whom we had prayed for each day.

Ginger's phone message said, "Billie, I left some roses for you on your front porch and I wanted to make sure you got them so you could bring them in before you go to bed. There is also a bud vase for your mom."

With this invitation I bounded to the front door and opened it with great expectation.

The sun had bid adieu and darkness had steeled its way with evening shadows still hovering around the lamppost lights outside.

There they were.

I picked up the large container of roses and then I saw the tiny bud vase as well.

Anxious to get them to the light inside, I flipped on the switch to the overhead in my kitchen area and ravished my gift.

Ginger had brought me a bucket of roses.

Mother had a bud vase.

I had a bucket.

It was a profusion of loveliness to behold.

Shades of vivid reds, lipstick, and rose, deep wine, and burgundy exploded; plush buttery yellows, warm apricot, burnished orange subdued; pinks in magenta, fuchsia and azalea intensified; palest ivory and creams tinged with a kiss of sunset hues blended.

All blended together integrating the palette of color with richness.

Their textures reminded me of velvet, translucent softness or opaque silk.

Mother's bud vase was filled with five ivory blossoms edged in a delicate mauve and tied with organza ribbon of the same color, elegantly arrayed.

One observation that captured me was this:

They were all open, completely full blown, fragrant, ready to be admired, enjoyed.
There were no buds.
A bucket of roses.
My senses were reinvigorated and my depleted soul breathed in the love of God,
Transformed by beauty.

We are being transformed into his likeness.... (1)

Our God wants us to be like HIM.
His beauty is visible like the rose but there are stages to unfold.
The tightly formed bud responds to the world of sunlight, water and air.
Day by day it becomes a beautiful rose.
As it unfolds the petals emit a fragrance.
His beauty is fragrant.

For we are to God the aroma of Christ...the fragrance of life. (2)

Our lives should be also.
His beauty is tangible.
HE said, *"It is I...touch me and see...."* (3)
Because His life was a sacrifice for ours we are transformed in it.
The incarnate, touchable Christ came so we might reach out and touch others
with "hands-on" love.
When the rose reaches its final maturity of bloom there is still more.
The petals fall and are crushed still releasing the fragrant life of the rose.

He was crushed for our iniquities. (4)

Crushed for our ugliness, our sin.
The Cross birthed our transformation.
Human hands cannot force the petals of a rose,
But we try.
There are no short cuts in the process of being transformed.
Beauty refreshes.
A bucket of roses lifted my sagging faith.
Beauty renews.
Reclaimed by God's love the will breathes in vitality.
Beauty remains.
God reproduces His life again and again and we continue to be transformed.
In this constancy we rest.

His work of transformation is intentional.
What will our response be?
The rose has thorns.
Life has potholes.
Choice is a choice.

Do not conform any longer to the pattern of this world but be transformed by the renewing of your mind. (5)

It is the renewing of our minds in Christ Jesus that develops godly, decisive people who adapt to change and form new habits which lead to beauty in behavior.

To be conformed or not to be conformed affects thorny thinking.
The writer Portia Nelson gives a five step demonstration in which we glean how choice shapes our lives.

Chapter One
I walk down the street.
There is a hole in the sidewalk.
I fall in.
I am lost…I am helpless.
It isn't my fault.
It takes forever to find a way out.

Chapter Two
I walk down the street.
There is a deep hole in the sidewalk.
I pretend I don't see it.
I fall in again.
I can't believe I am in this same place.
But, it isn't my fault.
It still takes a long time to get out.

Chapter Three
I walk down the same street.
There is a deep hole in the sidewalk.
I see it is there.
I still fall in…it is a habit…but, my eyes are open.
I know where I am.
It is *my* fault.
I get out immediately.

Chapter Four
I walk down the same street.
There is a deep hole in the sidewalk.
I walk around it.

Chapter Five
I walk down another street. (6)

Faith is a street.
I am accountable for where I go.
In the process I can change.
I can develop habits which will reflect the life of Christ.
How?
Because of the promise of His transforming power.

Being confident that he who began a good work in you will carry it on to completion until the day of Jesus Christ. (7)

HE promises to keep on transforming each of us day after day.

It was a November weekend that expressed itself with whistling trees shedding their foliage as they bowed down to the wind and clear cool nights visited by an intermittent autumn rain. The leaves had bedded down and were a colorful mat of fading brick, weathered gold, frail yellow and battered brown. They were a comfort to walk upon for the earth beneath was soggy. There was an inviting crispness to the air.
It was the breath of change.
Thanksgiving was a wink away and then, soon, Christmas would breathe upon us. I had looked forward to coming to northern New Jersey for a women's retreat. This was a wonderful group from Sayrewood. We were going to explore, together, a time of spiritual renewal. Since I realized that New York City was not far away, I had planned to have my daughter, Kellye, fly in and meet me afterward. Then she and I would spend a couple of days in New York City together – just for fun.
The time at the retreat was filled with a hunger for God's Word and a thirst for His presence. We had prepared in prayer and were met with His love flowing through all that was planned. There was true fellowship, music, good food, flourishing relationships, and challenges as we looked to find His way through the crossroads we all faced. Tears and laughter, hope and despair were exchanged as the bond of intimacy we shared in Christ Jesus unfolded like the

ruffled edges of a burnished claret autumn rose in all its beauty.
A pouring out and a pouring in was experienced.
We got beyond the thorns.
We experienced the unfolding of God's love.
When the last hug was given and we said goodbye, I was driven to my hotel.
Indeed I was consumed but it was the good kind of tired, an abiding satisfaction in doing what God has called me to do – to encourage.
There is a rest that follows the flow of Christ's empowering.

Christ in you (me), the hope of Glory (8)

Christ in me or you is the key.
Hope is respiration.
His Glory is a promise to us.
It is the embodiment of all of His attributes in perfect balance reflecting His character.
Words like magnificence, radiance and splendor tied to goodness, mercy, compassion and greatness come to mind, but they are incomplete.
The Glory of God is inexplicable but somehow able to be experienced.
How do I know?
I read it in God's Word.
Where HE equips, there is Glory.
I was anxious to go over details of the next phase of the week together with Kellye so I called her on the phone.
To my great disappointment, I found that she was ill with acute sinusitis and could not fly so she would not be able to come.
My hotel was prepaid for another two days so after discussing all of this with Roy, we decided I would rest and have my own personal retreat.
That's exactly what I did.
That Sunday night I ate a good meal in the hotel, soaked in a hot tub and the tension in my muscles melted. The sleep that followed was the sweet sleep of the beloved.

Let the beloved of the Lord rest secure. (9)

I always leave an open Bible in any room where I am staying as a reminder that God's Word dwells with me.
Monday was a lazy morning. Staying in my room I spent time studying in the Word, reflecting over the weekend and thanking God for His provision.
I needed an afternoon of walking for exercise so I discovered that a shuttle

would transport me to a mall and bring me back. By mid-afternoon I was feeling restored and began investigating the possibility of going into New York by myself to spend a day.

This was a bit bold for me but I talked with several folks in my hotel and by dinner I felt that I could figure out how to do it.

The final, concluding decision that remained was to seek God's direction in prayer. There were several factors: going and returning in daylight, feeling safe, learning about the transportation system, gauging my time, dressing comfortably and having a plan of what I might do.

To be honest, I just wanted a day in the Big Apple as an observer, just a relaxing rejuvenating time of God consciousness.

So I prayed for His peace as I went to sleep that night.

It would be the signal for me to go when I got up and it was.

In fact, I experienced more than peace in this prospect, there was the desire to seize with pleasure the venture prepared for me.

I love God's Encounters.

Sensing an expectancy and joy as I dressed, I began to pray that I would have His presence and protection throughout the day. I tucked my book PRAYERSURGE into my purse to give to someone if the opportunity presented itself and then charged downstairs to take the bus to Newark airport. My first challenge was how to buy a ticket. Would you believe a woman came up to me and asked me if I needed help? I eagerly said, "Yes, ma'am," and when I used these words, she knew I needed assistance.

A Southerner in New York isn't hard to spot.

When I told her what I wanted to do, she said, "Well, you probably should buy a round-trip ticket and that way you will already have your return ticket in hand when you board to come back to Newark." I thanked her and off I went. The ride to Penn Station took about forty minutes. Finding a window seat, I settled in and realized quickly that my Heavenly Father had planned for me to absorb this day in writing. The train lurched forward slowly at first and then picked up speed a bit before it began to come to the various stops along the way.

Pen in hand, I launched.

The day revealed glimpses of a gray overcast sky with hanging clouds.

Commuters flooded in with all kinds of belongings.

One man brought a bicycle which folded up conveniently.

A musician carried a violin case.

Computers, cell phones, head sets, palm pilots were abundant.

A charming wheelchair-bound older lady, pushed by a daughter who had the same Roman nose framing a happy tilted mouth, was intensely engrossed in conversation, which I thought might be Italian. They gestured a lot and laughed. They were accustomed to the train ride.

There were men in business suits with ties not quite tied, cups of coffee in one hand and a roll in another and one even had a hot dog at 8:30 am.

Protein is protein.

A couple of school-aged children, perhaps ages eight and ten, accompanied their mother getting on at one stop and exiting the next one just like clockwork.

There were the seasoned travelers who brought whatever they needed: thermos, shawl, lunch bag, even a small pillow.

Some carried books and newspapers.

During the first two stops, travelers were a bit talkative but then a familiar silence slipped in as all settled into the weary routine.

Soon many had dropped their head for a few zz's of rest before they had to depart.

I glanced at the countryside as it flew by, observing puffs of smoke in the distance from manufacturing businesses, small broken down poverty-stricken homes near the tracks, yet there were children playing nearby, stirring up life into this deprived scene. As we got closer to the city, we entered the tunnel that goes below the Hudson River.

The atmosphere changed.

People would merge into the train to find standing room. The platforms outside were overflowing with folks waiting. The walls behind them had posters detailing Broadway shows and other events. Finally, the last stop came and it was mine.

I couldn't wait to get off and get on with my city jaunt.

Penn Station is an underground covey of gift boutiques, food courts, restrooms, and book vendors. Suddenly the expulsion of folks exiting the train generated energy as everyone rushed to his destination.

When I walked up the steps from the underground station and saw the sunlight, it was a gratifying way for a gray day to slip away.

I looked around to get my bearings, to remember where I must return and then charged to find a diner for breakfast, for I was ravenously hungry.

At every traffic light hordes of folks paused to wait.

Finally I saw The Tick Tock diner.

I walked in, I sat down and ordered eggs, bacon, toast and coffee, one of the best breakfasts I have ever had and it cost $4.67.

But I had more, a view of city sidewalks from a perfect seat.

I watched people scurrying by as I ate.

They were all rushing to get to their destination.

Some were rushing and talking on cell phones as they walked.

Some did not have any place to go.

The street was their home so with faces smeared by despondency they looked vacantly at passersby who purposely passed them by.

One slender, tanned woman who had spiked orange hair with many gold earrings dangling to match the many bracelets on her arms towered over the group at the corner.

A family of four came to sit near me, there was a mother and dad and two children, perhaps in middle school, and of course, the kids were coaxed to eat all of their breakfast.

I breathed a prayer for all of these.

God knows all and wants all to know Him.

Then off I walked for several blocks to Macy's to get in my exercise, spending some time at the *Miracle on 34ᵗʰ Street* exhibit that was just being put together for the holiday season. The movie by the same name is a family favorite of ours.

Little Natalie Wood reminds us of Tatum, my daughter Kellye's youngest daughter.

It is a story of belief unfolding around the Christmas bustle found in a department store filled with tension, toys and deliberate good will.

The character Susie played by Natalie Wood hopes for a miracle and she gets it but she first has to learn to be a child again and dream.

And so do we.

Walking back toward Penn Station, passing the diner, I noticed a sign about the Empire State Building. I could not actually see it but wondered if it was in the area. Spying a Barnes and Noble book store, I dropped in for coffee.

Always, I have always wanted to see the Empire State Building. In fact, if Kellye had met with me on this trip, we might have planned it deliberately.

Yes, I was still pondering about going.

As I drank my coffee I whispered a prayer, "Lord is it possible that I am to go, even by myself?"

A pleasant looking young African-American man in his early twenties sat down beside me.

On impulse I turned to him and said, "Do you know how far away the Empire State Building is?"

He smiled a playful grin and said "yes, ma'am, I do. It is just around the corner."

"You're kidding," I said.

"No ma'am, would you like for me to take you to the corner and show you where it is?"

"Yes, I would!"

Out the door we went and lo and behold, there it was!

He then asked me if I had ever been to the Empire State Building before and I told him I had not.

Once again he started smiling and said, "You have got to go."

The fascination to go began to rise but I still felt a little uncertainty about going alone.

So I asked him if he felt it was safe for me to go alone.

He laughed out loud this time and said, "Yes, maam, just do it. Don't go home without going. You'll love it."

I knew then I was to go so I thanked him for his kindness to me and gave him my book on prayer and said, "Son, I have written a book on prayer because I live by prayer and faith in Jesus. I brought it along today to give to someone who might need encouragement. You have been so gracious to me and I would like for you to have it as a thank you. God Bless you. I am off to see the Empire State Building."

With that, he thanked me and we parted.

I had two city blocks to walk.

I was excited and still a bit hesitant, thinking to myself, my kids will never believe I went by myself to the Empire State building.

After I walked the first block I heard someone calling, "Mrs. Cash, Mrs. Cash, wait for me!"

I looked around and it was the young man I had just said goodbye to!

He was gasping for breath but he blurted out, "Mrs. Cash, I am a Christian. I need this book. I am in advertising here and am about to change jobs. I've been praying about this change. I'm from Richmond, Virginia. My folks just left and I took them to the Empire State Building when they were here. Thank you. Thank you, Mrs. Cash. I am walking you to the front door because I know you are supposed to go. My name is Cullen."

I then told Cullen that I lived in Tennessee.

He escorted me to the door and told the ticket folks, "Take good care of Mrs. Cash, who is visiting from Tennessee."

I thanked him again and said, "God bless you, Cullen."

Wow, what a God Encounter!

I bought my ticket and when I got into the elevator with lots of other folks, I took a deep breath as we ascended to the observation deck on the 86th floor. What a view!

The sunlight gloriously spilled in through the windows of the souvenir shop. The observation deck was packed with folks from around the world. I observed the intensity of interest; there was of a group of students in blue and white uniforms animatedly asking questions of a tour guide. A German couple was in line behind me on their first visit to America, a pair of young lovers were embracing around one of the view finders, an Asian professor on a sabbatical was taking notes and an adorable British lady was busy searching for the right postcard.

I had a monumental panoramic view of the city.

The skyline was a myriad of skyscrapers representing industry, apartment dwellings, theaters, restaurants, mom and pop businesses, banks, cathedrals, the states of New Jersey, Pennsylvania, Connecticut and even more....

Rivers and bridges surround this incredible city and on a clear day you can see for 80 miles.

To imagine the life of this metropolis was captivating.

New York, a melting pot of cultures, races, education and talent, is a city that significantly impacts our world.

What a privilege to be here this day.

I was enfolded by God's perspective.

When it was time to descend I was acutely aware of the small staircases that lead to the average-sized elevators that carried all of us down to the fist floor.

I began to think quietly upon the probable panic that must have erupted in crowded elevators and staircases on the day The Twin Towers fell, claiming the lives of nearly 3000 people.

Forever, the heartbeat of America was recalibrated.

People died.

People lived.

Their sacrifice transformed our country.

Some returned to their homes.

Some left for heaven.

All were known by God.

Grateful for my day in New York, I headed for Newark, ticket in hand.

The passengers seemed fatigued from their day's work.

Slumped into seats on the train, afternoon naps were taken.

Exhilarated and transformed by my serendipity, I was rested.

I was filled with praise and thanksgiving.

A southern mother in Richmond, Virginia might have prayed today for a son at a crossroads in New York City, and a southern mother from Tennessee was summoned by God to Cullen, to bring him a pillow.

Faith needs a cushion.

"Better a little faith, dearly won, better launched alone on the infinite bewilderment of truth, than perish on the splendid plenty of the richest creeds."

Henry Drummond

Our God listens to His children and orchestrates their way.

A heart that has made a home with Jesus can receive and believe.

Rekindled, faith soars.
God's music sang through me once again:

Revive us again.
Fill each heart with your love.
May each soul be rekindled with fire from above.
Hallelujah, Thine the glory.
Hallelujah Amen,
Hallelujah, Thine the glory
Revive us again.

Revived, life blooms.
His beauty prevails.

"If your eye is on the eternal, your intellect will grow...your actions will have a
beauty which no learning or combined advantages of other men can rival."
Ralph Waldo Emerson

God's beauty is a pillow of transformation.

My presence will go with you and I will give you rest. (10)

Rest in Him.

ARRESTING THOUGHTS

1.   Do you ask God to make plans for you?

2.   What keeps you from welcoming the adventure of living in Christ?

3.   Do you believe He is unfolding beauty for you this day?

REST ASSURED

"Surely my heart cannot truly rest, nor be entirely contented, until it rests in
Thee, and rises above all gifts and all creatures whatsoever."
– Thomas A Kempis

A PILLOW PRAYER

Faithful Father;
I cry out for YOUR perspective on life.
Why do I forget to be thankful?
When I am plotting, YOU are planning.
I must exchange my finite for YOUR infinite.
The beauty I crave is found in YOU.
The world of nature is found in YOU.
The transforming power to be, to live, to do is found in YOU.
YOU are beautiful, encompassing, creative, all knowing.
I forget to remember.
I repent again.
Thank YOU that with fresh awareness I must return gratitude for the blessing YOU have already provided.
Thank YOU for thorns, for unfolding, for fullness, for fragrance, for YOUR beauty.
These are stages in my faith journey
Transform me.
I rest my life in YOU alone, In Jesus' Name I come.

Chapter Thirteen

FINDING YOUR PILLOW

I found it.
Rest in HIM.

As a child I loved my pillow.
It was made from real feathers stuffed into a striped casing and it came from Mama Bella's farm house in Mississippi.
I don't remember when or how I got it but once I got it, I carried it with me everywhere.
Everywhere covers a lot of territory.
When I was anxious or lonely, my ritual was to cuddle my pillow and twist one corner of it with my thumb and forefinger over and over again.
Why this brought comfort I do not know,
But it did.
I now understand why dogs establish their scent.
In so doing they claim their territory.
I loved the smell of this pillow perhaps because it was my own or perhaps because it was the familiar resting place in the unfamiliar that ambushed my childhood.
I recall getting into the back seat of my parents' maroon Hudson Hornet automobile to go on a trip, with my pillow, and falling so contentedly fast asleep in its comfort that even a collision to the right side of the rear bumper didn't awaken me.
I attended so many schools from the first to the twelfth grade,
Thirty-three to be exact.
My pillow was a constant that traveled with me.
There were times it got misplaced in moves but I always found it.
Then one day I knew it had to go.
All the edges were frayed, for now tiny pure white feathers were sticking out.
I am sure it would be declared a true health hazard by today's standards.
Through the years, it had had all kinds of refurbishing, new ticking, double cases, even to the point of being repaired with needle and thread.

I clung to it through my early teens.

In the beginning years when my faith in God was fragile and untried, my tears, secrets, ambitions and dreams rested upon that pillow.

Then one day it dawned on me that the ever present contagious love of God through Jesus was daily to be my reality, truth, passion, my rest.

HE became my pillow.

Crossroads of faith intercept us.

Deciding to live for God is a decision toward the wholeness of holy living.

Choosing His way will require radical devotion.

There will be questions.

Is life about our best effort or is it about our living through God's best effort?

There will be surrender.

When we move toward His life as our model, it is a conscious power transfer which the world around us "dumbs down" as revolutionary.

It is.

There will be rest.

Living through Jesus is the call of transcendence.

It is upward faith, consummate, unparalleled because it rests on the finished work of the Cross.

We can add nothing.

We embrace His life as ours.

When Abraham began his trek of faith he knew God had expectations.

Obey.

Trust.

Build an altar.

Rest.

The pattern for living was given to God's people.

It has not changed.

We have.

We detoured by leaving the Word of God.

We diverted the Sabbath from a holy day to a help day.

We diminished life because we lost the rhythm of His rest.

We substituted work for worship.

We spurned Truth.

We lost our way to God.

But we can go home again.

Stand at the crossroads and look.
Ask for the ancient paths,
Ask for the good way and you will find rest for your souls

The quest for rest is still a search today.

Sometimes God causes us to pause and reflect upon an image that bears His providential imprint.

It was a marvelous May morning, a "God is in His heaven and all is right with the world" kind of morning.

Spring had sprung.

Purple and yellow petunias along the garden wall were vying for the sun's rays, which were like ribbons scattered across a sky so blue and clear that not a cloud dare intrude.

My husband, Roy, had gone outside to the patio to water some ferns thirsty for a drink and in a few moments he called to me, "Billie, come here, we have a robin's nest and there are three eggs in it!" I rushed outside and, sure enough, in the pink flowering crepe myrtle tree there was a nest in the fork of a two limbs.

What symmetry.

It was tightly woven, clean, and orderly and looked comfortable.

I had always heard the term "robin's egg blue" but since I had never seen a robin's egg I did not realize they really were blue.

It's a shade of blue that I've only seen in Easter egg dye.

How could eggs be birthed that color?

Suddenly, I was a child again and one of the missing spaces of my vagabond school years was being filled up to the brim.

I was about to embark on a life lesson that is perfectly natural in nature, a cycle encompassing biology, survival, provision, timing, and maturity.

There is an awe and wonder that surrounds creation.

There is a Creator who placed it there for us to see.

Roy and I marked our calendar to chart the progress.

We did not know how long the eggs had been there so we would have to carefully observe and wait.

Vicariously, we watched the parenting begin.

Sometimes the eggs would be in one position and then the next day they would be moved around.

Did the mother move them around or did they just roll around?

How long would it take to hatch these delicate little eggs?

My husband said that he thought it was between fourteen to sixteen days.

I looked it up.

He was right.

Apparently for our robin adventure it would be fourteen.

So, day by day, mother robin would sit on the nest preparing for the task of motherhood. She actually became accustomed to our snooping eyes as we strained to look.

When a severe thunderstorm hit and rain pelted the tree causing the limb to sway back and forth vehemently, I worried, but the mother bird knew what to do.

She would spread her wings and lift her tail so that water would gather on her back instead of the nest. The eggs were safe, protected and shielded from the weather.

The nest was a pillow.

Her body warmth was working the miracle of hatching.

There were times she would fly away but not too far.

The nest was always under surveillance.

A week later, Roy and I realized we had become completely absorbed in this event.

A little research revealed that it "takes from two to four days to make the nest with an average of 180 trips per day. The American robin can produce three successful broods in a year…the entire population turns over on average every six years." (1)

One morning I looked in at 7 am and there she was, still sitting on the nest but by 9 am there were three little baby robins with pink fuzzy bodies.

From this time forward until they were launched, both parents took turns guarding the nest. It was amazing what was required to feed them. They eat 35-40 meals a day.

A starling tried to interfere and there was a stand-off.

Don't mess with Mama's chicks.

The starling lost the battle.

Worms, fruits, small insects, all was fodder for open beaks begging to be fed.

The male and female take turns now to keep the fledglings warm.

Pin feathers emerge.

Most of the days, the babies sleep unless they are hungry and their chirping sounds are a reminder.

The days begin to roll by.

Roy kept the calendar.

By day nine downy feathers softened their wiry faces. It appeared as though they might be sleeping for their beaks would open and close in slow motion intermittently.

The days flew by and I realized soon they would be leaving the nest.

Walking outside one morning to check on them, I burst into song.

Did you know that robins are one of the first birds to sing in the morning and one of the last to sing at night? They are also one of the few to sing in the winter months.

How we need their song when we enter a stretch of unending pathos.
My praise poured out in one of the great hymns of the faith:

Oh Lord my God.
When I in awesome wonder
Consider all the worlds Thy hands have made.
I see the sky.
I hear the rolling thunder.
Thy power through the universe displayed.
Then sings my soul
My Savior God to Thee.
How Great Thou art.
How Great Thou art.
The sings my soul my Savior God to Thee.
How great Thou art.
How Great Thou art.

I thanked God for His incredible world.
Then without planning to do so, I began to talk out loud to my robins. I told
them, "You are getting ready to fly and I know you can do it."
Roy was watching me from inside the patio door, completely amused at how my
relationship and interest had piqued with our robin family.
It was a fresh discovery of God's creation.
Roy had hovered.
I had mothered.
I knew we both would miss them.
Time was flying.
We had begun to notice the little ones maturing and one day they got up the
courage to perch themselves at the edge of the nest.
Day Fourteen finally came.
The day for departure had come.
We got up early to see them but the third one had fallen out of the nest in its
attempt to follow after its siblings.
We saw him struggling on the ground with mother robin flying above noisily
chirping and swooping non-stop!
Surely it was her way of coaxing him to fly.
I walked outside and said, "Come on little bird, you can fly. Try again."
I stepped back inside for a moment to get my cup of coffee and Roy said, "Billie,
he did it."
And they were gone.

I felt sadness, fullness, release, completion.

The nest was empty.

Then I spoke out loud once more, "Dear robins, put the word out that we'll be waiting for another family to come and build a nest."

We had participated in watching a miracle in nature mirror the mighty provision of a Creator God.

What did I see?

My porcelain music box had come to life.

If HE could orchestrate life for the birds of the air, from birth to maturity with all the checks and balances needed to survive, HE will show us the way to live in harmony and health as we reclaim His rhythm of rest.

We must.

When I began this book, I knew there would be challenges.

God always tests us on what we think, speak, write and live.

My husband retired for the second time and we sold a home and moved to Collierville, Tennessee.

Our son sold his home in Virginia and moved to Italy.

My mother sold her home and moved around the corner from us.

Within a thirteen-month period I participated in the moving preparation, organization and redecorating of all these homes.

Giving away, throwing away, keeping, and seeking, organizing and agonizing, ministering and questioning.

Then the health crises of my mother began, between the closing on her Cordova home and the move to her new home in Collierville.

Every time she broke a bone, we were broken.

God gave us weights we could not carry alone.

The exhaustion of manual labor,

The emotional depletion,

The fatigue of faith,

The downward spiral of disappointment,

And finally the cry for rest.

HE began to carry me in ways I had not known.

I rediscovered some ancient paths, the good way.

When I did, I found rest, His.

We delete the good without realizing it until we are dead ended.

We deviate and lose our way home.

Home has a highway.

And a highway will be there; it will be called the Way of Holiness…only the redeemed will walk there, and the ransomed of the Lord will return.

They will enter Zion with singing. Everlasting joy will crown their heads.
Gladness and joy will overtake them and sorrow and sighing will flee away. (2)

There is an eternal rest.

If I go and prepare a place for you, I will come back and take you to be with me. (3)

God is always preparing our way.

"I know not! Oh, I know not!
What joys await us there! What radiancy of glory!
What bliss beyond compare!"
Bernard of Cluny

A gladdened assurance,
Heavenly rest is a promise.
Earthly rest is a divine proviso.

Some books stir us toward self help, awareness.
Some are scholarly and school us with more knowledge.
Some warn.
In Jeremiah 6:16 we have looked at a holy admonition:
Stand, look, ask, walk, find.
What?
Rest for your soul.
As the chapter continues, God speaks.

To whom can I speak and give warning?
Who will listen to me? (4)

The people responded.

We will not listen. (5)

Are you listening, dear reader?
If you have traveled this far with me, perhaps you are listening.
We bottom out when we leave God out.
We find no rest without HIM.
You and I need a pillow.
I found mine.

The one the Lord loves rests between his shoulders. (6)

Our work on earth prepares us for heaven.

With rich insight the renowned Victor Hugo describes his life's work as he anticipates eternal rest:
"I feel within me a future life. I am like a forest that has been razed; the new shoots are stronger and brighter. I shall most certainly rise toward the heavens...the nearer my approach to the end; the plainer is the sound of immortal symphonies of worlds which invite me. For half a century I have been translating my thoughts into prose and verse: history, philosophy, drama, romance, tradition, satire, ode and song; all of these I have tried. But I feel I haven't given an utterance to the thousandth part of what lies within me. When I go to the grave I can say, as others have said, 'My day's work is done.' But I cannot say, 'My life's work is done.' My work will recommence the next morning. The tomb is not a blind alley; it is a thoroughfare."(7)

Get your pillow.

Make straight in the wilderness a highway for our God. (8)

I'll meet you on the highway.

The following prayer was my heart's desire for this book.

Oh, Lord my God, sometimes I am brought low and completely spent because I have not known the way to YOUR rest.
Life can be overwhelming.
There is much to do.
The hours flee.
The pressures increase
And yet when I stop and look for YOU,
I find YOU waiting on me.
How humbling, how forgiving.
There are crossroads to face, but I must be still to recognize them.
Stir me to ask for the paths that have proven true, the ancient paths.
Ancient is not archaic,
It is the authentic.
I want to walk the good way.
Doesn't everyone?

Point me to the pattern found in the Word.

How many times I have substituted my way for the *good* way, which is YOURS.

Mine is only a fleeting reprieve, temporal, dissipating.

I hunger for rest that renews and replenishes my soul.

So, I come.

I bow down.

I stand. I look. I ask. I walk.

I find.

YOU are my guide, my path, my pillow.

Open my understanding to this timeless Truth with words chosen from YOUR WORD.

Write them through me and draw others who are weary of their own search to lay down their plans and take up YOURS.

Only then will they find rest for their souls.

We all need a pillow on the highway.

As a pilgrim seeking the *good* way, resting in Jesus' Name I pray.

Billie Cash
Collierville, TN
Summer 2007

REST ASSURED

"Thou art the Lord, who slept upon the pillow,
Thou art the Lord who soothed the furious sea.
What matter beating wind and tossing billow
If only we are in the boat with Thee?
Hold us quiet through age-long minute
While Thou art silent, the wind is shrill:
Can the boat sink while Thou, dear Lord art in it?
Can the heart faint that waiteth on Thy will?"
– Amy Carmichael

SOUL REST

Shepherd of my soul.
I come.
YOUR love for me has been proven again and again.
YOU are constant.
I have wandered far from the good way.
Forgive my presumption, my reckless ambition, and my wayward view.
I lost my pillow.
I purpose to return to YOUR provision.
I repent.
I reclaim
YOUR
Reverence, Embrace, Sufficiency, Transformation.
I will remember the stories of faith found in the Bible.
Renew my heart.
Restore my joy.
Refresh my soul.
The highway awaits me.
I found my pillow.
In YOU ALONE
I rest.

ABOUT THE AUTHOR

Billie Cash is an international retreat and conference speaker/musician. She has authored four other books, Windows of Assurance, Light Breaking Through, Autumn Rain and PRAYERSURGE. With humor and insight, she brings accountability. A fresh authenticity and personal application are the keys to her ministry.

Billie Cash
278 W. Colbert St.
Collierville, TN 38017
Website www.billiecash.com
E-mail: brcash@comcast.net

I would love to hear from you!

NOTES

CHAPTER ONE

1. II Corinthians 1:20 NKJV
2. I Corinthians 2:9 NKJV
3. Psalm 127:2 KJV
4. Psalm 32:8 NKJV
5. I Chronicles 16:24a
6. *Lessin, Solum*: Roy Lessin and Heather Solum, *The Comfort of Rest and Reassurance* (Uhrichsville: Barbour) 2005, p.33

CHAPTER TWO

1. http://www.stressdirections.com/personal/about_stress/stress_statistics p. 1
2. *Masiach and Leiter*: Christina Maslach and Michael Leiter, *The Truth about Burnout* http://www.christainity.ca/faith/Christian/Christian-living/2003/11.004.html p. 3
3. Matthew 11:28 The Message
4. Matthew 11:28 NIV
5. http://apolloguide.com/mov_fullrev.asp?CID=3470$Specific+4172 p, 2
6. *Springsteen*: Anne Springsteen, *It's Me O Lord*, (St. Louis: Concordia, 1970) pp 24-25
7. *Buchanan*: Mark Buchanan, *The Rest Of God*, (Nashville: W Publishing, 2006) p.17

CHAPTER THREE

1. *L'Engle*: Madeleine L'Engle, *The Ordering of Love*, (Colorado Springs: Shaw Books, 2005) p.186
2. Genesis 12:1
3. Genesis 12:2
4. Joshua 24:2
5. Hebrews 11:8-9
6. Genesis 12:7
7. Genesis 12:11b-13
8. Genesis 13:14-17
9. Genesis 15:6
10. Genesis 16:11
11. Genesis 16:13
12. Genesis 18:14
13. Genesis 20:12
14. Genesis: 21:18,20
15. Genesis 22:8a

16. Genesis 22:12
17. *Wilson:* Dr. Ralph Wilson, *Disciple Lessons from the Faith of Abraham* http://www.jesuswalk.com/ebooks/abraham.htm
18. Isaiah 46:8-10b,11b
19. *Bell:* Rob Bell, *Velvet Elvis,* (Grand Rapids: Zondervan, 2005) p. 59
20. *Kimmel:* Tim Kimmel, *Little House on the Freeway,* (Sisters: Multnomah, 1994) p. 97
21. Malachi 3:16 NKJV

CHAPTER FOUR

1. I Peter 4:11b
2. Psalm 95:1a, 2
3. I Peter 3:11b
4. *Yancy/Schaap:* Philip Yancy and James Calvin Schaap, *More Than Words,* (Grand Rapids: Baker, 2002) p. 50
5. Psalm 16:9
6. *Helms:* Hal Helms, *Echoes of Eternity,* (Brewster: Paraclete, 1996) p. 2
7. Philippians 2:10-11
8. *Prince:* Derek Prince, *Entering The Presence of God,* (Charlotte: Whitaker House, 2007) p. 37

CHAPTER FIVE

1. Lamentations 1:3b
2. Lamentations 1:14b
3. Lamentations 1:18a
4. Lamentations 2:11b
5. Lamentations 2:19
6. Lamentations 2:17
7. Lamentations 3:22-23
8. Lamentations 5:19-22
9. http://www.alcoholfreechildren.org/en/text/stats/society.cfm Grant B, Dawson D, Stinson F, et al.2004. The 12-month Prevalence and Trends in DSM-IV Abuse and Dependence: Unites States, 1991-1992 and 2001-2002. Drug and Alcohol Dependence 74 (3): 223:234.
10. http://www.teendrugabuse.us/teen_drug_use.html p. 1
11. http://www.annecollins.com/obesity/statistics-obesity.htm p. 1, Wellness International Network Ltd.
12. *Barna:* Barna Research Group, *Morality Continue to Decay,* 3 November, 2003.
13. http://www.wmich.edu/destinys-end/statistics.htm Boyer and James, 1983 p. 131.
14. Isaiah 48:17b
15. Romans 11:22
16. Psalm 107:1
17. *Buchanan:* Mark Buchanan, *The Rest Of God,* (Nashville: W Publishing, 2006) p. 63
18. Psalm 107:9, 13
19. Psalm 107:11-12
20. Psalm 107:43
21. *Packer:* J I Packer, *Knowing God,* (Downers Grove: InterVarsity Press, 1977) p. 150
22. *Colson:* Charles Colson, *The Good Life,* (Carol Stream: Tyndale House, 2005) p. 33
23. *Pamuk:* Orhan Pamuk, *Snow,* (New York: Vintage, 2004) p. 4

CHAPTER SIX

1. Ecclesiastes 1:15
2. Ecclesiastes 1:18
3. Ecclesiastes 2:10
4. Ecclesiastes 2:21
5. Ecclesiastes 9:1b
6. Ecclesiastes 9:17
7. Ecclesiastes 10:2
8. Ecclesiastes 10:4b
9. Ecclesiastes 12:13
10. Psalm 19:7
11. Psalm 85:6
12. Hebrews 4:12
13. Psalm 107:20
14. John 14:14
15. John 15:7
16. Matthew 7:7
17. Mark 11:24
18. Mark 9:23
19. Hebrews 11:1
20. Deuteronomy 20:4
21. *Nowen:* Henri J.M. Nowen, *The Dance of Life* (Notre Dame: Ave Maria, 2005) p. 30
22. *Yancy/Brand:* Philip Yancy and Dr. Paul Brand, *In The Likeness of God,* (Grand Rapids: Zondervan, 2004) p. 19

CHAPTER SEVEN

1. *Guinness:* Michele Guinness, *Genius of Guinness,* (Ambassador: Greenville, 2005) p. 136
2. II Corinthians 12:9

CHAPTER EIGHT

1. http://www.backyardnature.net/earthwrm.htm
2. http://www.floridabenedictines.com/aboutus.html
3. Psalm 85:6
4. *Merton:* Thomas Merton, *The Seven Story Mountain* (New York: Harcourt Brace, 1948) p. 410
5. Acts 17:27b

CHAPTER NINE

1. Jeremiah 9:23
2. Isaiah 49:16
3. Jeremiah 31:3

4. Leviticus 20:26
5. Exodus 31:12
6. Hebrews 4:9
7. *Baab*: Lynne M. Baab, *Sabbath Keeping* (Downers Grove: InterVarsity, 2005) p. 125
8. John 12:32
9. *Postema*: Don Postema, *Catch Your Breath*, (Grand Rapids: CRC, 1997) pp. 32-33
10. Proverbs 13:12
11. Hebrews 3:7-11
12. *Prince*: Derek Prince, *Entering the Presence of God* (Charlotte: Whittaker House, 1984) p. 46
13. Isaiah 42:10b,12 (NASB)

CHAPTER TEN

1. James 4:6
2. Hebrews 13:9
3. Hebrews 12:15
4. II Timothy 2:1
5. Psalm 119:42
6. *Cash*: Billie Cash, *PRAYERSURGE* (Greenville: Ambassador, 2005) p. 92
7. John1:17
8. I Chronicles 29:17a
9. Isaiah 32:18
10. Psalm 91:4
11. *McMenamin*: Cindi McMenamin, *When Women Long for Rest* (Eugene: Harvest House, 2004) p. 121
12. II Peter 3:18
13. http://www.desiringgod.org/ResourceLibrary/sermons/By/Date/1986/
14. II Corinthians 6:14a
15. *Moore*: Beth Moore and friends, *Voices of the Faithful* (Brentwood: Integrity, 2005) p. 126

CHAPTER ELEVEN

1. Psalm 90:12
2. Psalm 103:19
3. Exodus 19:4
4. I Corinthians 15:26
5. I Thessalonians 4:17
6. Psalm 46:1, 2 a, 7
7. Job 38:22-23
8. Daniel 4:25c
9. Genesis 29:17
10. Genesis 29:26
11. Genesis 29: 31
12. Colossians 2:10
13. *Frangipane*: Francis Frangipane, *The Stronghold of God* (Lake Mary: Charisma, 1998) p. 76
14. Deuteronomy 17:19

15. Genesis 49:31
16. Psalm 4:8

CHAPTER TWELVE

1. II Corinthians 3:18b
2. II Corinthians 2:15a,16c
3. Luke 24:39b
4. Isaiah 53:5b
5. Romans12:2a
6. *Nelson*: Portia Nelson, *There's a Hole in My Sidewalk: The Romance of Self Discovery* (Hillsboro: Beyond Words, 1994) pp. 2-3
7. Philippians 1:6
8. Colossians 1:27
9. Deuteronomy 33:12a
10. Exodus 33:14

CHAPTER THIRTEEN

1. http://www.i-pets.com/rpet19.html
2. Isaiah 35:8a,9b, 10
3. John 14:3
4. Jeremiah 6:10
5. Jeremiah 6:17b
6. Deuteronomy 33:12c
7. *Hugo*: Victor Hugo, *The Future Life* quoted by David Wilkerson, "And I Shall Dwell," sermon preached Moorpark, California, February 18, 20. http://www.moorparkpres.org/sermons/2001/021801.htm
8. Isaiah 40:3b

OTHER BOOKS BY THE AUTHOR

WINDOWS OF ASSURANCE

In her Journey of Prayer, Billie Cash shares the resources she used to persevere as a school girl in 33 different schools. Those experiences propelled Billie into the artificial light of the theater; but it was the penetrating light of God's presence that birthed identity and ready resolve. For each window she opened, His love met her with grace and called her to test the real release of prevailing prayer.

ISBN: 1 889893 59 5

$12.99/£8.99 (224 pp)

LIGHT BREAKING THROUGH

Light. *The visible reminder of Invisible Light.* (T. S. Eliot) The light of God searches all things, our struggles, loneliness and brokenness. This book lets us experience that light, as it breaks through our struggles, intercepting us with truth, love, and fresh insights at every turn, in every season. He urges us onward, to continue, to grow, to believe, to love, and to finish our race, giving us illumination in the darkest days. We can trust His Light.

ISBN: 1 889893 97 8

$9.99/£6.99 (144 pp)

AUTUMN RAIN

This book is a message of faith's journey, having a beginning, becoming dependent, being responsible, fruitful and then transforming the landscape through transplanted lives. The metaphor of the garden is carried throughout the book; beginning faith is nurtured by Spring rain but transforming faith has a harvest, an abundance brought by the autumn rain, the rain of harvest. It is a faith that continues to change the landscape of life.

ISBN: 1 932307 33 8

$11.99/£7.99 (224 pp)

PRAYERSURGE

Billie writes as she lives – in bursts of glorious energy. With her concise, almost poetic style, she pulls us into this beautiful description of the work of prayer in a Christian's life. Her heart for God is revealed. Be careful as you read – this is a short book but the message is large – hear the call! Rise up in prayer! Love God! Love others! Be transformed!

ISBN: 1 932307 41 9

$10.99/£8.99 (160 pp)